WITCHCRAFT AND MAGIC IN SIXTEENTH- AND SEVENTEENTH-CENTURY EUROPE

Studies in European History

General Editor: Richard Overy
Editorial Consultants: John Breuilly
Roy Porter

PUBLISHED TITLES

Peter Burke The Renaissance
William Doyle The Ancien Regime
Geoffrey Scarre Witchcraft and Magic in Sixteenth- and Seventeenth-Century Europe
R.W. Scribner The German Reformation
Robert Service The Russian Revolution

FORTHCOMING

T.W. Blanning The French Revolution
Brendan Bradshaw The Counter Reformation
Michael Dockrill The Cold War 1945–1963
Geoffrey Ellis The Napoleonic Empire
R.J. Geary Labour Politics 1900–1930
Mark Greengrass Calvinism in Early Modern Europe
Henry Kamen Golden Age Spain
Richard Mackenney The City State and Urban Liberties, 1450–1650
Roger Price The Revolutions of 1848
Clive Trebilcock Problems in European Industrialisation 1800–1914

WITCHCRAFT AND MAGIC IN SIXTEENTH- AND SEVENTEENTH- CENTURY EUROPE

GEOFFREY SCARRE
Tutor in Philosophy
University of Durham

HUMANITIES PRESS INTERNATIONAL, INC.
Atlantic Highlands, NJ

First published in 1987 in the United States of America by
HUMANITIES PRESS INTERNATIONAL, INC.,
Atlantic Highlands, NJ 07716

© Geoffrey Scarre, 1987
  Reprinted 1988, 1990

Library of Congress Cataloging-in-Publication Data
Scarre, Geoffrey.
  Witchcraft and magic in sixteenth and seventeenth
century Europe.
    (Studies in European history)
    Bibliography: p.
    Includes index.
    1. Witchcraft—Europe—History—16th century.
2. Witchcraft—Europe—History—17th century.
3. Magic—Europe—History—16th century. 4. Magic—
Europe—History—17th century. I. Title. II. Series:
Studies in European history (Atlantic Highlands, N.J.)
BF1584.E9S23   1987   133.4'3'094   86–27399
ISBN 0–391–03505–3 (pbk.)

Printed in the United States of America

Contents

Acknowledgements

I should like to thank Dr Richard Overy, the Series Editor, for helpful comments on an earlier draft of this essay. I am grateful also to the Reverend Edward Featherstone for some suggestions and references on demonology, and to other friends and colleagues who for many months have listened to much about magic and witchcraft.

Note on References

References in the text within square brackets relate to items in the Select Bibliography, with page numbers in italics, for example [76: *122*].

List of Tables

Editor's Preface

The main purpose of this new series of studies is to make available to teacher and student alike developments in a field of history that has become increasingly specialised with the sheer volume of new research and literature now produced. These studies are designed to present the 'state of the debate' on important themes and episodes in European history since the sixteenth century, presented in a clear and critical way by someone who is closely concerned himself with the debate in question.

The studies are not intended to be read as extended bibliographical essays, though each will contain a detailed guide to further reading which will lead students and the general reader quickly to key publications. Each book carries its own interpretation and conclusions, while locating the discussion firmly in the centre of the current issues as historians see them. It is intended that the series will introduce students to historical approaches which are in some cases very new and which, in the normal course of things, would take many years to filter down into the textbooks and school histories. I hope it will demonstrate some of the excitement historians, like scientists, feel as they work away in the vanguard of their subject.

The format of the series conforms closely with that of the companion volumes of studies in economic and social history which has already established a major reputation since its inception in 1968. Both series have an important contribution to make in publicising what it is that historians are doing and in making history more open and accessible. It is vital for history to communicate if it is to survive.

R. J. OVERY

1 Witchcraft and Magic

A belief in the reality of witchcraft and magic is not a component of the average modern Westerner's view of the world. For most of us, the idea that human beings can harness occult forces to serve their good or ill purposes is as defunct as the notion of a flat earth, and as unlikely to be resuscitated. When misfortune strikes us, we do not search our neighbourhood for the old woman who has bewitched us; nor do we believe that knowledge or love or power can be ours if we employ the correct rites, charms or incantations. The witch and the magician are absent from the stage of real life, and have been relegated firmly to the realm of fantastic fiction.

It has not always been so – and it is not so even now in parts of the non-Western world. Many technologically undeveloped societies retain beliefs in witches and sorcerers with significant similarities to those of Europeans of the early modern period. But there is something peculiarly tragic and poignant about the history of the witch belief in Europe. In a span of two hundred years or so, beginning in the later fifteenth century, a great many people, most of them women, were prosecuted for witchcraft, and of those found guilty it is possible that 100 000 suffered a capital penalty. Some of those accused doubtless did attempt to harm their enemies by occult means, and thus were guilty of witchcraft at least in intention. Yet we now recognise that the alleged crimes of the witches were mostly impossible – a witch could conceivably invoke the Devil, but she could not fly through the air to meet him, nor harm her neighbours by evil magic.

Historians have long taken an interest in early modern beliefs in witchcraft and magic and their terrible consequences, but the last twenty years in particular have seen a spate of publications in this area which has greatly improved our understanding of it. An important feature of much of this recent writing has been the substantial use made of research in other academic disciplines, such as anthropology and sociology, to help explain the historical phenomena. As a result of this broadened perspective, together with a great deal of painstaking analysis of court records and other archival material bearing on the social and economic status of those accused of witchcraft and of their accusers, a more sophisticated picture is emerging than was available previously. Few writers today incline to echo the views of such rationalist historians as Lecky, Hansen and Lea, who regarded the beliefs of sixteenth- and seventeenth-century people in witchcraft as wholly irrational superstitions, and thundered with moral indignation against the credulity and cruelty of witch hunters and judges. 'There are no pages of human history more filled with horror than those which record the witch-madness of three centuries, from the fifteenth to the eighteenth', wrote Lea [56: *xxx*]. The advance of research has done nothing to mitigate the sense of horror one feels on reading the grim records of trials, tortures and executions, but it has done much to remove the impression that the only proper explanation of witch prosecution is to be found in the madness or the badness of the prosecutors.

There were, to be sure, isolated figures even in the sixteenth century who voiced scepticism about the prosecution of witchcraft. The essayist Montaigne observed that: 'It is putting a very high price on one's conjectures to roast a man alive for them.' In England, Reginald Scot wrote in 1584 that those who regard themselves as able to do harm by occult means are merely deluded, whilst Johann Weyer, physician to the Duke of Cleves, argued that old women who believe themselves to be witches are suffering from over-powerful imaginations – though he added that their abnormal mental states are caused by the Devil. Such views, however, were those of a minority of writers. Among educated men close to 1600 there was a tendency to believe that witchcraft was not only real, but increasing in seriousness daily. King James VI of Scotland complained in 1597 of the 'fearefull abounding at this time in this Countrey, of these detestable slaves of the

Divel, the Witches or enchaunters', who were 'never so rife in these parts, as they are now'. In 1613, Pierre de Lancre, who had burnt about eighty people for witchcraft in the French–Spanish border region, expressed the view that the progress of witchcraft in that area was now unstoppable, and that the sect of witches had infiltrated itself into the Basque population at large. Some years earlier, in 1580, Jean Bodin, one of the most formidable intellects of his day, had declared that sorcerers are driven by a veritable 'demon-mania' to run after devils and do their bidding, and that such crimes, which are both atrocious and widespread, need to be energetically met with the most grievous punishments.

But just what are witchcraft, sorcery and magic? If a discussion of these in their sixteenth- and seventeenth-century context is to be fruitful, it is first necessary to characterise them with some precision.

[i] Witchcraft and sorcery

Witchcraft and sorcery are clearly closely related in that both involve occult causality – that is, they are taken to operate not through the familiar cause–effect mechanisms of everyday life, but through certain hidden, mystical means. But many anthropologists, following Evans-Pritchard's work among the Sudanese Azande [27], believe that a distinction should be drawn between them. Witchcraft, on their conception, is an internal power some people possess, an inborn property which they inherit, just as they may inherit the properties of being right-handed or snub-nosed. Witches can harm other human beings, their animals or crops, without performing any special acts; they can cause damage merely by a look or a malicious thought, and sometimes may even do so involuntarily. Sorcerers, on the other hand, have no such innate capacity for occult harm, but employ magical operations, such as chanting spells or performing certain ritual operations, to accomplish their ends. In principle, anyone can become a sorcerer by learning the appropriate techniques, whereas to be a witch it is necessary to be born one. A sorcerer wishing to hurt someone might use a verbal formula whilst damaging some-

3

thing belonging to the intended victim, such as a piece of his clothing, or some hair or nail parings, relying on mystical relationships between those objects and their owner magically to transfer the harm to him; but a witch can achieve a similar objective without so much as lifting a finger.

Historians, however, have mostly been dubious whether this distinction has much application to the European scene. There was, as Thomas has pointed out, some belief in the existence of people who had the 'evil eye', able to harm men or animals simply by looking at them [99: 553]. And Henningsen has suggested that Evans-Pritchard's contrast was captured in the Spanish distinction between *hechicería* (sorcery) and *brujería* (witchcraft) [43: 10]. But trial records provide little evidence that two classes of offenders were singled out on these lines; the *modus operandi* of the accused witch seems normally to have been of little interest to accusers or court officials. French historians thus have much justification for using the one term *sorcier* to cover all those charged with causing harm – or *maleficium*, as it was termed – by occult means. In England, courts were more concerned to determine what *maleficia* the defendant was guilty of than how she had produced them, while on the Continent and in Scotland the focus of attention tended to be on the defendant's relations with the Devil. It remains possible that in some parts of Europe a greater measure of distinction between witchcraft and sorcery may have been made at a popular level than is apparent from the surviving records; but on the basis of the available evidence, it assists the historian little to hold the two terms sharply apart.

Typical *maleficia* which figure in European trials include procuring the deaths and sickness of people and animals, spoiling crops, causing sexual impotence, raising bad weather, and interfering with the manufacture of butter, cheese and beer. Such *maleficia* had been feared in rural areas of Europe from immemorial antiquity, and while there was nothing in principle to limit the practice of black magic to the country-side, it appears on the whole to have loomed less large in the perspective of urban dwellers. But occult forces could also be enlisted to serve non-malicious ends. 'White witches' and wizards – in England often called 'cunning folk' or 'blessing

4

witches', and in France *devins-guérisseurs* – existed in many communities, and would for a fee attempt the magical curing of diseases, counter malign sorcery, identify one's enemies, foretell the future, and locate treasure or lost property. It is likely that such practitioners of white witchcraft often satisfied their clients by purely non-occult means, though to attract custom they may have deliberately cultivated an air of personal mystique. Many were undoubtedly familiar with folk-remedies and herbal lore, whilst such divinatory tasks as the identification of enemies would not have proved insuperable to someone with an acute ear for local gossip, or who was well provided with suitable informants. Often, indeed, one man's white witch might have been another man's black. Muchembled has suggested that while clients might confidently approach a *guérisseuse* in a distant village, those who lived in her vicinity may have feared her powers and, if occasion arose, denounced her as a maleficent witch [77: *112–15*]. It is likely, too, that some of these consultants genuinely believed they had the power to do either good or ill by occult means.

But for many educated people of the sixteenth and seventeenth centuries, these characterisations of white and black witchcraft would unquestionably seem to have left out the most important element. Orthodox learned opinion, promoted by religious and increasingly accepted by secular authorities, had it that witches or sorcerers were in league with that great foe of God and mankind, the Devil, and were utilising his superhuman powers for their own operations. This concept of witchcraft as a manifestation of diabolical power seems to have had less grip on the popular than on the learned mind. Examinations of court records over the last few years have amassed great support for the view that unlearned people were not especially concerned with witchcraft as a devilish thing; like many people today in non-Western cultures, they accepted that the world contained hidden forces which knowing individuals can tap, just as anyone can tap the more familiar forces of everyday life, without speculating as to their origin. The typical peasant who laid an accusation of witchcraft did so because he believed he had suffered injury from a witch, not because he

5

looked on her as a servant of the Devil.

Following Larner [53: 7], we may describe as 'primary witchcraft' the witchcraft or sorcery of *maleficium* which frightened the European peasant and which continues to frighten people in many societies at the present day. But it was much less the notion of *maleficium* than a concept of the witch as a follower of the Devil that had foremost place in the minds of theologians and many witch judges; and inevitably, therefore, the term 'witch' in the present essay will often bear this extra demonological connotation. A *sorcier*, wrote Bodin, 'is one who by diabolical means knowingly attempts to accomplish some end'. This overlay of a demonological content on the idea of primary witchcraft is distinctively European, and is possible only within a Christian culture.

[ii] Low magic and high magic

Using spells and rituals to kill or maim a man or his beasts, to spoil a neighbour's butter-making, to cause the water from a well to be foul, to produce good or bad weather, to make Jack fall in love with Jill – all these are examples of *low magic*, which is closely associated with Larner's 'primary witchcraft' and with what anthropologists call 'sorcery', though it was not necessarily directed to evil ends. Low magic, essentially practical in intention, was the magic of uneducated white and black village witches or sorcerers, and of their often only slightly more cultivated urban counterparts. Theoretically unsophisticated, it was a magic rooted in folk traditions orally transmitted from one generation to the next, many of its spells and prescriptions having their origin in the most distant antiquity.

But in early modern Europe, magic was by no means the exclusive preserve of ill-educated low magicians. Far removed from low magic in its theoretical and operational sophistication was the *high magic* of the Renaissance magus, a learned and visionary figure combining elements of the scientist and the priest, and entranced by the noble prospect of man controlling the cosmos by magical means. For such men as Marsilio Ficino (1433–99) and Pico della Mirandola

(1463–94), it was through magic that humanity could realise its highest aspirations to understand and to compel the forces that govern the universe, and to make its nearest approach to divinity. Renaissance high magic rested firmly on the quasi-mystical philosophy of Neoplatonism, which had originated in third-century Alexandrian speculation on the meaning of certain strands in the thought of Plato. Influential too were the so-called Hermetic writings, themselves actually a product of the Neoplatonist tradition, but believed before they were correctly dated in the seventeenth century to be the works of an Egyptian sage contemporary with Moses, named Hermes Trismegistus. Medieval magicians had had some knowledge of the Neoplatonist–Hermetic tradition, largely filtered through Arab sources, but high magic received a considerable boost during the Renaissance from the rediscovery of Hermetic manuscripts, and from the new enthusiasm for reading the works of the ancients.

High magic depended on a complex theory, in which astrological and alchemical notions were mingled, of the world as a mystically interconnected system, and the magician believed that this interconnectedness (the 'concord of the world', as Ficino termed it) could be exploited to produce results on earth by certain kinds of ceremonies and incantations. Crucial to this conception was the Neoplatonist idea of the *spiritus mundi*, the spirit of the world, which infuses all things and is the medium through which the influence of the stars is drawn down to earth. The purpose of magic then becomes that of attracting benign stellar influences and hindering malign ones; and the magician must study how to compel these forces by carving images on stones (talismans), chanting and singing mystical songs, making certain gestures and producing appropriate odours – all of these at astrologically propitious times. The spiritual unity of the world is the ground of the 'sympathies' among its parts which are the magician's concern. To illustrate the nature of this unity, Ficino cited the well-known phenomenon of sympathetic vibration: just as plucking one taut string of a lyre will cause a second string to vibrate in sympathy with it, so are all parts of the universe linked together in a single harmonious rhythm, which enables the magician who performs the correct actions

7

to capture and use the powers of the heavenly bodies. For instance, to fight a fever, according to Ficino, 'one sculpts Mercury in marble, in the hour of Mercury, when Mercury is rising, in the form of a man who bears arrows' [36: 75].

There was much debate about the extent to which high magic relied on demons. Even St Thomas Aquinas, the arbiter of orthodoxy, had not forbidden the use of natural substances which, by virtue of astral correspondences, might have a certain efficacy – occult certainly, yet still strictly within the bounds of the natural – to produce some result; for example a particular plain stone, placed on the skin, might in this manner help to cure some disease. But Renaissance high magic, with its acceptance of the Hermetic doctrine of a universe animated in all its parts, and with the tendency of some of its exponents in their more poetical flights to talk of 'planetary deities', invited the charge that it was not really a natural magic but rather a demonically facilitated one, and as such reprehensible. Some theorists, such as Henry Cornelius Agrippa (1486–1535), were actually willing to admit that their magic in some of its aspects employed demonic power, but insisted that only good demons, or 'angels', were involved. Whatever the sincerity of this plea, high magic was understandably greatly suspect in the eyes of the ecclesiastical authorities.

The intellectual defences offered for magic by Renaissance Neoplatonism enabled it to retain the belief of many members of the educated classes through the early modern period. Popular low magic at the same time continued to thrive as it had always done, seemingly little indebted to the writings of the learned, though more or less garbled echoes of the thought of Pico or Agrippa occasionally appeared in manuscript manuals of practical magic. Some of the men and women who plied the magic trade professionally undoubtedly had some smattering of learning, yet there can have been few white wizards and wise women even among the urban practitioners who had much grasp of the subtleties of the Neoplatonist cosmology. In England, as Thomas has shown, wizards were generally artisans, or sometimes farmers, merchants or clerics, and practised magic only in their spare time [99: 295–6]; for the most part they can have taken little interest in the theoretical basis of magic, though presumably few were inclined to attribute its efficacy to the Devil. Some of these consultants built up considerable practices and charged high fees. Their clients were not confined exclusively to lower-class people: high-ranking members of society too sometimes required a magic cure for illness or sought to learn the future by divination. Magical remedies were in fact available for an enormous range of problems. In 1544, Lord Neville was promised the assistance of magic in his attempts to become proficient on the lute and virginals, while in the late seventeenth century the antiquary Elias Ashmole employed astrological talismans to rid his house of rats and mice [99: 275, 759].

[iii] Other perspectives on witchcraft and magic

The fact that witchcraft and magic have lost their reality for educated people in the modern West contributes to the difficulty of understanding their significance in the Europe of the sixteenth and seventeenth centuries. Hence historians do well to pay careful attention to those researches of scholars working in other disciplines which throw light on the nature of witchcraft and magic.

Most important among the disciplines on which historians have drawn for enlightenment has been anthropology. We saw, it is true, that a distinction between witchcraft and sorcery that anthropologists have found relevant to some societies is of limited application to the European experience; and this provides a warning that it is unwise to assume that witch beliefs will take a uniform shape in all those cultures in which they are found. Nevertheless, the influence of anthropology has been an extremely fruitful one, as it has led many historians to consider the European material in relation to various hypotheses about the origin, direction and social impact of witchcraft accusations which have been proposed by anthropologists investigating technologically undeveloped societies. (For witchcraft in contemporary societies see, for instance, [27, 63, 65].) The combination of insights taken from anthropology with deft use of the methods of sociological

9

analysis has produced much new understanding of the social contexts in which witchcraft was practised, and accusations of harmful magic laid; such an approach is well illustrated in the important studies [53, 59, 77, 99], which will receive discussion below; [7], an able and exhaustive discussion of the 1692 outbreak of witch hunting at Salem, Massachusetts, brings a similar perspective to bear on a single locality. Anthropological and sociological modes of enquiry have, in ways we shall examine, righted an imbalance found in much of the older writing about European witchcraft and magic, which inclined to concentrate too exclusively on the ideas of contemporary theorists, and neglected the study of the social environment of witch trials.

Historians of witchcraft can also in principle learn from psychology, though there has not yet been an impressive quantity of high-quality modern writing devoted to the psychological explanation of witchcraft phenomena. Modern knowledge of such disorders as hysteria and schizophrenia should help to explain why some people quite sincerely believed they attended witches' sabbats or were possessed by devils, and why some (including children on many occasions) felt an urge to accuse innocent persons of bewitching them. Psychologists can also offer assistance in understanding the virulent hatred of women that informed some of the treatises on witchcraft produced in the fifteenth to seventeenth centuries. The history of witchcraft offers, in fact, a rich field for the student of abnormal psychology, and there is no doubt that the historian and the psychologist could reap mutual benefit from a pooling of their knowledge. There is actually nothing new about the idea that psychological theory has a contribution to make to the understanding of witchcraft; as early as the sixteenth century there were those of a sceptical turn who argued that people who believed they flew through the air or danced with the Devil were afflicted by melancholy, or suffered from a diseased imagination. Much scope remains for present-day psychology to continue this tradition, and throw further light on the mental states of victims and accusers in the witch-prosecuting centuries [34, 101, 112].

There are important questions about the rationality of beliefs in witchcraft and magic that invite the assistance of

10

another discipline, philosophy, though not many historians working in this area have so far made much direct use of philosophical writings; Larner is perhaps the most notable exception [53, 54]. As we saw, writers in the past usually condemned the beliefs that sustained the witch trials as absurd and unjustifiable, and those who held them as credulous and superstitious fanatics. There is considerable recognition now that this attitude was simplistic and unfair, but this change of outlook places extra pressure on the historian to think philosophically about the conditions under which a system of beliefs is rational. A belief need not be irrational simply because it is false; it is false, for instance, that the sun goes round the earth, but it was not irrational to believe this before the evidence for heliocentrism was available. Yet if we do not wish to allow that there are no irrational beliefs at all, we must insist that the rational ones measure up to certain standards of acceptability, and are supported by evidence of an appropriate sort. But what we take to be good evidence is very largely dependent on what theories about the world we are already disposed to accept, and it is this fact which makes it so peculiarly difficult for us to assess the rationality of beliefs that belong to a picture of the world markedly different from our own. People believed in witchcraft when they believed, as we do not, in a universe pervaded by a variety of spiritual forces of a personal kind, both good and evil. A satisfactory theory of evidence should be neither so restrictive that it rules as irrational all beliefs that fail to fit with our modern Western view of reality, nor so liberal that it construes as rational any beliefs whatsoever. Interesting discussions of the grounds on which rationality can be ascribed or refused to beliefs and practices deeply at variance with our own can be found in [38, 58, 85, 108].

Help of a somewhat different sort is available from pharmacology and toxicology, which can throw light on the real possibility that narcotic ointments were responsible for at least some of the strange experiences, including that of flying through the air to the witches' meetings, that some witch suspects confessed to with apparent sincerity. Sixteenth- and seventeenth-century writers often referred to the use of 'witch salves', and some even conducted experiments to test their

11

efficacy at producing wild dreams [31, 35, 40].

Lastly, the development of women's studies over the last few years has prompted some fresh thinking about one of the most difficult questions to be faced by the historian of witch-craft – the question, namely, of why women constituted about 80 per cent of accused witches. While the striking preponderance of women among trial defendants has long intrigued historians, recent work on the historical experience of women in male-dominated European societies has provided a sounder basis on which to attempt explanations, though much still remains dark. Such studies as those by Fraser, Kelso, Maclean and Monter have helped to elucidate the status of women, in theory and in practice, in early modern times [33, 48, 62, 74]. The feminist pamphlet of Ehrenreich and English is stimulating, but is, as we shall see, implausible in its main contention that witches were women healers disliked by the male establishment [23].

2   Witchcraft, Magic and the Law

[i] Development of the learned stereotype of the witch

The concept of the witch held by many churchmen and literate lay-people in the sixteenth and seventeenth centuries was a synthesis of a number of elements, some of them of considerable antiquity. The most ancient ingredient in the mix that defined the witch was the notion of harmful magic, which can be traced back to the remotest historical times. Practitioners of evil magic attracted heavy legal penalties in the Greek and Roman worlds, and again in the early medieval kingdoms.

Then there were various traditions of women who flew by night, on wicked or at least on mysterious errands. The Roman *strix* was thought to be a woman who could transform herself into a bird of owl-like form, and who delighted to feast on human flesh; there is a famous literary presentation of a flying *strix* in Apuleius' novel *The Golden Ass*. Somewhat less sinister were popular beliefs, condemned by the Church as remnants of paganism, in women who rode out at night with a goddess, variously referred to as Diana, Herodias, Holda, Perchta and by numerous other local names. Such aerial cavalcades, often taken to be composed of the souls of the dead as well as of living women, were believed in some parts of Europe to be concerned with punishing wrong-doers and rewarding the virtuous, but they were naturally the object of some fear to the peasantry, and it is likely that there was a tendency for these 'ladies of the night' to become confused with the *strix* variety of night-flyer. It has been suggested by Rose, without hard evidence yet not without a grain of plausibility, that stories of the night-ride with Diana may have had their origin in some real nocturnal ride or ceremony in later pagan times [89: *110*].

The Church was keen to condemn all such traditions as superstitious and pagan. A key document in this context, because for several centuries regarded as having conciliar authority, is the so-called *Canon Episcopi*, which though believed to have issued from the Council of Ancyra (314), was probably no older than the ninth century, and may have been part of a lost capitulary. The *Canon Episcopi* denied the reality of the night-ride with Diana, and declared that those women who believed that they rode with her were the victims of a devilish delusion. Whatever its actual origins, the *Canon Episcopi* was a typical product of the official Church policy of placing a demonological interpretation on beliefs it held to be pagan; in a similar way, all pagan deities were identified with demons.

The science of demons, or demonology, was largely a medieval creation, though it looked to the Bible to sanction its basic claims. In fact, biblical demonology is obscure and doubtfully consistent (see [47]), thus allowing great scope for interpretation by the Fathers and Doctors of the Church. Origen in the third century declared that all magic was possible only through the agency of demons, but it was orthodox to stress, as Augustine and, later, Aquinas did, that the Devil and his subordinate demons operated only with God's permission. As it was the Devil's aim to spite God and to procure the damnation of mankind, it was a nice question, and a much discussed one, why God should allow him to exercise his evil powers. A standard, if not wholly satisfactory, answer was that God wished to give men a chance to use their free will to choose between virtue and vice; and so he permitted Satan, as the Pseudo-Bernardus said, *tentare servos Dei* – to tempt the servants of God. According to this thinking, to abandon God and throw in one's lot with the demons, in return for the opportunity to utilise their marvellous powers for one's own ends, was supremely wicked, whilst being one of the greatest temptations that Satan could offer.

It was not generally believed that demons – and consequently the human beings who practised magic through their aid – were capable by their own powers of working true miracles outside the course of nature, which only God could perform. But if demons were restricted to operating by natural forces, they could nonetheless through their great knowledge and abilities create effects far beyond anything that unaided human beings could achieve: as Alexander of Hales put it in the thirteenth century, they could not work *miracula*, but they could work *mira* (wonders). With such powers, demons were a source of much fear to medieval and early modern people; a man striving to save his soul from damnation was engaged in a chess contest against a much cleverer opponent, and he could only hope to win if he threw himself upon divine protection. 'The Devil', wrote the late-fifteenth-century preacher Paulus Wann, voicing the widespread contemporary anxiety, 'is most subtle in intellect, highly astute in his malice, most swift in his motion, unremitting in doing harm, insatiable in damning, implacable, invisible, horrible to think upon and impossible to restrain.' Against such a foe, the Church needed to mobilise all its forces.

The Church's fear and loathing of religious dissent undoubtedly owed much to the thought that dissenters, or heretics, were weakening its power to combat the Devil, and were indeed servants of the great enemy. It is significant that a more resolutely repressive policy on heresy began in the High Middle Ages simultaneously with a growth in concern with the Devil; at the first burning for heresy, at Orléans in 1022, the charges included holding secret orgies at night and worshipping the Devil in the form of a black man [92: 87]. Naturally enough, the conviction that all heresy had a demonic inspiration led to a certain sameness in the accusations levelled against heretics, whether Reformists, Cathars, Waldensians, Fraticelli or whatever, and the same charges were eventually, in the fifteenth century, to reappear in the trials of those other deviants, the witches. The learned stereotype of the witch that the early modern era inherited from the late Middle Ages incorporated many of the horrific features that had previously been ascribed to heretics. Witches, like heretics before them, were accused of meeting together at night in secret places, feasting on the flesh of infants, holding orgiastic revels (often involving sexual intercourse with demons) and worshipping Satan. Above all, they were

15

held guilty of making a pact with him, whereby they promised to become his creatures and do his bidding in return for temporal goods or demonic assistance in their evil schemes. In one respect, however, the stereotype of the witch was importantly innovatory: while heretics could be of either sex and of any age, it became normal to expect witches to be women, and generally elderly ones.

Scholars are generally agreed that the major elements in the learned conception of the witch, whilst they had been known earlier, converged to define this new enemy of God only in the course of the fifteenth century. The new synthesis encountered some objection from those who claimed that it ran counter to the authority of the *Canon Episcopi*, but it became common to respond that what the *Canon* forbade was belief in the reality of the night-flight with a goddess, not the belief in the flying activities of witches. The witch's heretic-like allegiance to Satan was what explained her capacity for maleficent sorcery, and it also marked her out in the Church's eyes as someone with a quite universal hatred for all Christian people. As such, she merited harsher treatment than had normally been meted out to magicians in the Middle Ages who, while being subject to secular penalties if they attempted *maleficium*, were not in general seen as implacable foes to God and mankind. Aquinas had taught that high magic must normally involve, explicitly or implicitly, a pact with the Devil, and in 1326 the papal Bull *Super Illius Specula* was issued against the very suspect practice of ritual magic; but magicians were mostly thought of, and probably thought of themselves, as attempting to coerce demons while remaining good Christians, rather than as recruits to the Satanic army. The influential Hugh of St Victor in the twelfth century considered that the appropriate treatment for magicians was not death, but expulsion from the community of the faithful. Some magicians, such as the famous Cecco d'Ascoli in Florence in 1322, were executed; but the discreet magician's survival chances, particularly before the fifteenth century, were reasonably good.

The formation of the concept of demonic witchcraft owed much to the writings and practices of Inquisitors. The papal Inquisition had developed gradually from the twelfth century, and was directed at the suppression of heresy. In pursuit of its objective, it adopted special legal procedures including the withholding of the identity of the witnesses from the accused, the admission of evidence from those not normally thought fit to testify, the refusal to allow the accused legal representation, and torture. Whilst there was some debate about the meaning of the term 'heresy' (did it cover only beliefs, or did it extend to actions too?), in the course of the fourteenth century it became largely accepted that the making of demonic pacts fell within the jurisdiction of the Inquisition. This brought magic within its purview, and in the fifteenth century, by a consistent if novel development of their theory of magic, Inquisitors began to press the charge of diabolic pact even against unsophisticated village practitioners of maleficent magic – against those, in other words, characterised by Larner as 'primary witches'. Secular jurisdictions in some areas took up the concept of demonic witchcraft, and likewise inquisitorial methods for dealing with it.

Kieckhefer has ably explored the manner in which, in the fifteenth century, learned notions were superimposed on popular, traditional ideas at trials for maleficent magic. Thus in trials at Todi (1428) and Cologne (1456), the emphasis was diverted from the original charges, respectively, of love magic and weather magic, to fresh ones of using an ointment made from dead infants and of diabolism [49: 73–4]. Inquisitorial technique, with its set formularies of interrogation, tended to make it difficult for an accused person to be seen in any other light than that in which his judges had determined to regard him. There is no more than a little exaggeration in Russell's statement that: 'The Inquisitors were taught what to look for, and they almost always found it, whether it existed or not' [92: 159].

Maleficent sorcery, as a secular offence, was subject to legal proceedings throughout the medieval period and, as in any crime of violence, the penalty was generally in proportion to the severity of the harm the defendant was believed to have caused. But the fully-fledged stereotype of the demonic witch, that was to prove so catastrophic to so many, was not in operation in trials before the fifteenth century: Cohn has suggested that it can first be perceived in trials in the Swiss

17

canton of Valais in 1428 [14: *225*]. In the next few years, trials for witchcraft run by the Inquisition in the French Alps, which had initially been seeking out Waldensian heretics, reinforced the connection between the stereotypes of witchcraft and of heresy (in fact, one French term for witchcraft is *vauderie*, which originally signified the Waldensian heresy). The devil-worshipping, cannibalistic, evil-doing witch is now revealed in her full horror; and as Cohn has rightly said, the addition to the mix of the characteristic of nocturnal flight meant that there now opened up the prospect of great assemblies of witches: and thus of a maleficent *witch sect* [14: *227–9*]. Testifying to the anti-Semitic tendencies of the age, the meetings of witches were commonly designated by Hebrew terms, initially being called 'synagogues', and later 'sabbats' (or 'sabbaths').

The fifteenth century saw the first rash of theoretical disquisitions on witchcraft and its appropriate treatment – a genre that was to burgeon in the two succeeding centuries. Such works as Nider's *Formicarius* (*c.* 1435), the *Errores Gazariorum* (*c.* 1450), Jacquier's *Flagellum Haereticorum Fascinariorum* (1450s), Molitor's *De Lamiis* (1489), and, most famous of all, the lubricious *Malleus Maleficarum* or 'Hammer of Witches' (1487) by the Dominican Inquisitors Institoris and Sprenger, helped to disseminate the new ideas about witchcraft, a process facilitated by the invention of printing in the middle of the century. The availability of printed treatises on witchcraft no doubt played some part in stimulating the interest of literate people in the subject, but it would be unreasonable to lay too much responsibility on the printing press for the witch prosecutions of early modern times; had the press not existed, the new theories of witchcraft would have been transmitted in manuscript or by word of mouth as theories had been transmitted in the Middle Ages, and would eventually have reached the same audience, if more slowly. That printing caused the European witch hunt to be much worse than it would otherwise have been has not been satisfactorily established, though further research is needed before a firm assessment of the impact of printing on prosecution can be attempted.

[ii] Witch prosecution: regional survey

It will never be possible to know with certainty how many people in Europe were prosecuted for witchcraft, or how many suffered death or some lesser penalty after conviction. Scrupulous records of proceedings were not kept in all localities, and of those which were, many have been lost. Much material, however, remains in the archives awaiting examination, and it is probable that ideas of the scale of witch prosecution will undergo further refinement in the future. Sufficient work has already been done in recent years to indicate that earlier guesses at the number of deaths for witchcraft (often based on the reading of sensational pamphlet accounts of trials, rather than on archival research) have been exaggerated. It is no longer believed that many hundreds of thousands died for witchcraft. In so far as the sporadic nature of witch prosecution permits inductive extrapolation from what statistics are known, it seems reasonable to suggest a maximum figure of 100 000 executions, disregarding a wholly unknown number of unofficial lynchings of suspected witches.

Whilst prosecutions for witchcraft were an endemic feature of life in large parts of Europe for many years, from time to time certain areas experienced witch hunts of greatly increased intensity. These occurred when the authorities became persuaded that witches existed in numbers great enough to form a dangerous secret conspiracy against the community in which they were living, and from which they had to be uprooted. Such scares or panics, often though not exclusively town-based, were enabled to develop by the use of torture to extract from luckless suspects the names of their 'accomplices'; as the torture was frequently extremely severe, it took a spirit of rare endurance to resist the pressure to accuse other innocent people of witchcraft, who could then be arrested and tortured in their turn. A curious fact about these witch scares, that historians are trying to explain, is that they are rare in the first century or so after the stereotype of demonic witchcraft had reached its final form. Despite having its conceptual roots in the Middle Ages, witch prosecution is an early modern, not a medieval, phenomenon, with some of the worst panics datable to the 1590s, the years around 1630 and the 1660s.

The territories of the Holy Roman Empire were variously afflicted by witch trials, some having a great many. Monter thinks that the Swiss Confederation may have executed some 5000 for witchcraft, and Austria only slightly fewer [76: *130*]. Some parts of Germany, such as southern Bavaria and the Lower Rhine region, had relatively few scares; others, including Lotharingia (1000-plus executions), Westphalia (800), Schaumburg-Lippe (500-plus), the Electorate of Trier (many hundreds), Würzburg (900), Bamberg (300-plus), Freising, Strasbourg and Fulda were less fortunate (see [93]). Midelfort's detailed research in southwestern Germany (modern Baden-Württemberg) has uncovered records of 3229 executions of witches between 1561 and 1670, trials of up to ten people a year accounting for 31 per cent of this total, and large panic trials of more than twenty people per annum 40 per cent [70: *32, 71–2*]. A German town in the grip of a witch scare was the scene of some terrifying spectacles; thus a chronicler could write of Wolfenbüttel in Brunswick in 1590: 'The place of execution looked like a small wood from the number of the stakes.' At the western edge of the Empire, Lorraine and Franche-Comté suffered some severe bouts of witch prosecution. The judge and demonologist Nicolas Remy claimed to have burnt 900 witches in Lorraine in the 1580s and 1590s, though that figure may have been exaggerated for cautionary effect. In Franche-Comté another judge-cum-demonologist, Henri Boguet, stimulated a policy of severity at the beginning of the seventeenth century, and there were bad panics in 1628–9 and again in 1657–9 (see [76]). Waves of panic occurred in the Duchy of Luxembourg, then under Spanish rule, in the periods 1580–1600 and 1615–30; 358 people are known to have been executed for witchcraft in those parts of the Duchy for which records have survived (see [21]). Namur in the Low Countries is known to have contributed close on 200 victims between 1509 and 1646 (according to [78]). The experience of the Empire demonstrates that once the habit of energetic witch prosecution had taken hold of an area, it could easily spread to other areas: zeal for prosecuting witches was infectious.

In France, if one excludes Lorraine and Franche-Comté (which only became permanently subject to the French crown during the wars of Louis XIV after 1660), the areas most badly affected by witch trials were the Pyrenees, Languedoc, the Alps and the North East. Muchembled has located the climax of prosecuting zeal in the years 1580–1610, when the Pyrenees in particular suffered very badly, and further waves of trials occurred in the late 1630s in Burgundy, Champagne, Languedoc and other places, and around 1670 in Normandy, Béarn and Guyenne [77: *290–5*]; the trials of the third wave were, significantly, ended by royal intervention [64: *457–8*]. On the whole, and always excepting Lorraine, France suffered less severely than Germany did, and there were fewer trials involving large numbers of defendants. Statistics for France are frequently uncertain; in one area investigated in detail, corresponding to the modern Département of the Nord, and known to have had relatively many trials for witchcraft and related magical offences, around 140 people are believed to have been executed, most of these in the peak periods 1591–1600, 1611–20 and 1651–60 (see [78]). A striking feature of the French experience of witchcraft was a fashion for bewitched convents, the most famous instances being at Aix (1611), Loudun (1634) and Louvais (1633–44). In all these cases, a priest was burnt for having caused devils to enter the bodies of nuns or young girls, though there was much contemporary debate as to whether the 'victims' were really possessed, merely feigning or mentally ill [45, 64].

Both Italy and Spain, the heartlands of the Inquisition, saw surprisingly few witchcraft trials, with the peak of prosecutions being over as early as 1550. What trials there were tended to take place in the northern parts of these countries, close to borders with other witch-hunting regions, possibly indicating a heightened popular consciousness of witchcraft there. Thus Venetian territory witnessed a considerable number of trials, and there were sharp persecutions in the Spanish Basque country in 1507, 1517, the 1520s and (as a spillover from the bad scare on the French side of the Pyrenees then) in 1610. The Inquisitions in Spain and Italy, which had become exceedingly painstaking in their legal procedures, seem to have grasped earlier than most other jurisdictions the scale of the difficulty of obtaining satisfactory proof that an accused person was a witch; they appear, too, to have been doubtful whether witchcraft was common. Accordingly, they acted with great circumspection in response to accusations of witchcraft, and made efforts to ensure that local secular authorities did the same [43].

Official zeal for exterminating witches had largely evaporated in Spain and Italy before it had even begun to appear in certain other lands. Poland had its worst period of witch panics as late as 1675–1720, and mass trials continued for years after. Hungary, too, suffered badly in the eighteenth century, and one contemporary report speaks of thirty-four people being burnt for storm-raising in 1728–9 (see [56: *1252–3*]). In the north, Sweden's greatest scares took place after 1650, the most notorious incident occurring at Mohra in Dalecarlia in 1668–9, when several children accused a number of women of taking them to the sabbat; as a result of these charges, a sizeable though uncertain number of women were burnt (seventy, according to [5: *207–8*]). Swedish-speaking areas of Finland knew some trouble in the same period, but by and large other parts of Scandinavia were free of large-scale trials.

Also largely unscathed by witch prosecution were Catholic Ireland and Calvinist Holland, the former remote from the main currents of European thought and affairs, the latter in their very forefront. Ireland knew a mere handful of trials for witchcraft, and these without pronounced demonic elements, while Holland burnt its last witch in 1610 [43: *22*]. Muscovite Russia likewise was apparently free of major witch panics, though Zguta has shown that a fear of primary witchcraft was strong in all ranks of society from the Tsar downwards, and has uncovered records of the trials of ninety-nine persons for this offence in Moscow between 1622 and 1700 [111]. In only one of the Moscow trials is there any reference to the accused rejecting God and accepting Satan as master [111: *1204*]; and indeed the Western concept of demonic witchcraft scarcely penetrated to the world of Orthodox Christianity.

England's experience of witch prosecution was in important respects different from that of much of Continental Europe.

In English trials, the emphasis of the charge normally fell on the *maleficia* allegedly performed by the supposed witch, rather than on any contract with the Devil, although invoking demons was forbidden by statute in 1563, and making a diabolic pact in 1604. The sabbat at which the Devil presides is virtually unheard of before the Essex trials of 1645 promoted by the witch-finder Matthew Hopkins; the meetings that the witches of Pendle in Lancashire were said to attend in 1612 were merely feasts, without the presence of Satan. But a common charge against English witches, though much less often raised against their Continental counterparts, was that they kept 'familiars' – imps or demons in the form usually of small animals such as dogs, cats and toads, which did their bidding in return for nourishment from a special nipple concealed on the witch's body, and known as her 'witch-mark'. (This 'witch-mark' is not to be confused with the 'Devil's mark' of Continental witches, an insensitive point in the body produced by Satan as a sign of compact.) Normally an accused witch was searched carefully for any mole, spot or blemish that could be identified as her witch-mark, and such a mark, not surprisingly, was often found.

Multiple trials were considerably less common in England than in mainland Europe, probably because of the absence of the notion of witches gathering in groups at the sabbats, and the non-employment of torture to extract from accused people the names of accomplices. Most cases coming before assizes or quarter sessions concerned individuals indicted for more or less serious *maleficia*; strictly, acts of white witchcraft were also subject to punishment by the secular courts, but generally the 'cunning folk' who performed them ran more risk of being presented before ecclesiastical courts, which could impose a variety of penances. The work of Ewen, Kittredge and Macfarlane has shown that the later years of Elizabeth's reign marked the climax of witchcraft prosecutions at assizes and quarter sessions. In Essex, which Macfarlane has studied in detail, the 1580s and 1590s saw the rate of indictments rise to its peak, and between 1560 and 1680 overall 5 per cent of all criminal proceedings at Essex Assizes were for witchcraft – a high figure probably reflecting an unusual degree of concern in that county with witchcraft

[59: *28–30*]. The number of executions in England as a whole is not known, but is extremely unlikely to have exceeded one thousand; Macfarlane considers three hundred a probable maximum [59: *62*].

In strong contrast to England, Scotland – or, to be more precise, the lowland areas of Scotland – pursued witches with a ferocity scarcely surpassed in any Continental centre. In Scotland, as in Germany or France, the witch was regarded as a monstrous criminal who had committed the ultimate treason by rejecting God and entering into a compact with the Devil, and secular and religious authorities alike were keen to hunt her down. According to Larner's authoritative research, the bulk of prosecutions in Scotland occurred between 1590 and 1662, with peaks in 1590–1, 1597, 1629–30, 1649 and 1661–2 [53: *60*]. Fife and the Lothians were the most badly affected areas, while some centres of population, such as Prestonpans, Inverkeithing and, further south, Dumfries, repeatedly suffered witch scares. With a much smaller population than England's, Scotland nevertheless executed far more people for witchcraft: Larner estimates the figure at between 1000 and 1600 executions up to 1706 [53: *73*].

New England, it is interesting to note, had proportionately fewer executions for witchcraft than even Old England had. The panic at Salem, Massachusetts, in 1692, which resulted in nineteen executions, has haunted the American consciousness ever since, but in fact was quite exceptional. Witch prosecution was not a feature of life in the New England colonies, and it is unlikely that the total of executions for the offence reached thirty.

[iii] Witch prosecution: the victims

Women were accused of witchcraft far more commonly than men. King James thought that there were twenty female witches to every male, because the female sex was frailer than the male, and therefore 'easier to be intrapped in these gross snares of the divell'. To what extent misogyny, or at least a low estimate of women's power to resist evil, was responsible

24

Table 1: The proportion of women among defendants at witchcraft trials

Location	Women tried (%)	Location	Women tried (%)
Basel	95	Geneva	76
Essex	92	Franche-Comté	76
Namur (Belgium)	92	Saarland	72
S. W. Germany	82	Castile (Inquisition)	71
Dept. du Nord	82	Freiburg (Switzerland)	64
Venice (Inquisition)	78	Waadtland (Switzerland)	58
Ostrobothnia (Finland)	78	Moscow (seventeenth century)	33

Sources: [70, 76, 78, 93, 111].

for stimulating the prosecution of women as witches is a matter we shall investigate more fully in the next chapter; but there is no doubt that in most of Europe the stereotypical witch was a woman, and usually an old and poor one.

Records suggest that in Europe as a whole, about 80 per cent of trial defendants were women, though the ratio of women to men charged with the offence varied from place to place, and often, too, in one place over a period of time. Neglecting temporal variations, Table 1 presents the percentage of women among persons tried for witchcraft at a number of sample locations.

It can be seen from Table 1 that while in some places a far from negligible proportion of defendants were men, for the most part the stereotype of the female witch held up fairly well. The most striking exception to the general pattern is provided in the seventeenth-century Moscow trials analysed by Zguta, where two-thirds of the defendants were men; here, clearly, there was no disposition to look on witchcraft as essentially a woman's crime.

In most of Europe, witches were not merely generally expected to be women: they were also thought most likely to be old or elderly ones. Defendants against witchcraft charges were typically over rather than under 50. Thus in Essex, women between 50 and 70 appear most commonly in court records, while Monter has shown that in the Geneva trials of 1571–2 the median age of the accused was 60 [59: *162*; 76: *122*]. An often noticed feature of the records is the large number of widows among the defendants; for example in Neuchâtel 44, in Essex 42 and in Toul (Lorraine) 58 per cent of accused women were widows. This high proportion of widows may to some extent indicate the increased chance that a solitary woman ran of being suspected of witchcraft, but it is also a reflection of the fact that male mortality rates were higher than female (see [71: *47*), so that many women within the most likely age range for accusation had already outlived their husbands. Another category of often solitary women, spinsters, also appear with some frequency among defendants. It has been suggested (for instance in [70: *184–5*]) that spinsters, like widows, were at risk partly because they appeared to offer a threat to the patriarchal family; but it should be noted that in early modern Europe as many as 15 per cent of women remained permanently unmarried [71: *70*], and there were therefore many spinsters in most communities. Moreover, unmarried women, who had avoided the hazard and stress of multiple child-bearing, had a higher chance than married women of living to the age at which the danger of accusation became greatest.

Poverty was a further hallmark of the witch. Except during some of the large Continental panics when customary notions of who might be a witch tended to disintegrate, people accused of witchcraft came mainly from the lower socio-economic groups. Moralists believed that those without wealth were most likely to succumb to devilish temptations to witchcraft, which offered them an irresistible prospect of avenging their wrongs, becoming rich and obtaining power over their neighbours. But there is evidence that accused witches were less commonly at the bottom of the social heap than a little way above it; often they belonged to families that were on their way down through the social structure, and they may have embarrassed and annoyed their more successful neighbours by their complaints and demands for assistance [59, 99]. The typical witch was the wife or widow of an agricultural labourer or small tenant farmer, and she was well known for a quarrelsome and aggressive nature. In

26

addition, in some parts of Europe that prosecuted witches with great vigour, particularly the Empire, various other kinds of low-class people perceived as moral derelicts occasionally attracted accusations of witchcraft, such as thieves and highway robbers, fornicators and homosexuals. Evidently the guiding thought here was that someone who was guilty of one gross moral crime might well be guilty of the grossest of all, and have made a compact with Satan.

In times of severe panic, however, the usual limitations could be breached, and all manner of men and women be accused of witchcraft, including high-ranking (though rarely noble) members of society. Where torture was used, as it commonly was, to force accused witches to provide the names of others who had been with them at the sabbat, a chain reaction was set in motion that could deliver into the hands of the witch judges persons of considerable social prominence and respectability. Such was the terrible experience of the city of Ellwangen in southwestern Germany in 1611–12. Beginning with a woman of 70 who was tortured into confessing to witchcraft, many people were condemned and executed after being forced into naming accomplices in a savage process which reached further and further up the social ladder. Once some priests had been condemned, it was no longer clear who could and who could not be a witch; some people even seem to have made spontaneous confessions of their own guilt. In 1611 some 100 were executed, then a further 160 in the following year. A judge who protested after his wife was accused and executed was himself tortured and executed in November 1611. One observer commented in that year that if condemnations went on at the same rate, the city would soon be depopulated. After 1612, trials continued at a somewhat lower tempo until 1618, when they ceased. (For the panic at Ellwangen and others in southwestern Germany, see [70].)

It is incontrovertible that the use of torture played a large role in the genesis and escalation of panics. Witchcraft being regarded as an essentially secret crime as well as a very serious one, authorities felt justified in employing the strappado, the heated chair, vices for the arms and legs, thumbscrews and other painful devices to uncover the truth. A sustained refusal to admit one's guilt normally led to the dropping of charges, but few were able to withstand severe and prolonged torture without confessing what they thought their interrogators wanted to hear. A woman at Nördlingen who refused to confess through fifty-six sessions of torture perhaps set a record for endurance; happily, she was finally released at the insistence of the authorities at Ulm [56: *1087*]. Not so ultimately fortunate was a 57-year-old woman of Styria in 1673, who died insane after being forced to kneel on a sharp-pronged torture stool for eleven days and nights, with burning sulphur applied to her feet, in order to make her confess to a demonic pact [87: *32*]. The desperate plight of such victims is movingly expressed in a passage from a letter to his daughter which Johannes Junius, the former bürgermeister of Bamberg, smuggled out of his prison in that city after his arrest for witchcraft in 1628: 'Innocent have I come into prison, innocent have I been tortured, innocent must I die. For whoever comes into the witch prison must become a witch or be tortured until he invents something out of his head and – God pity him – bethinks him of something' (for the full text of the letter see [72]).

Sometimes the dissolution of the conventional notion of the witch as an elderly woman proceeded so far that even children were punished for witchcraft. Rather more commonly, children accused other people of bewitching them, and there are well-known cases from several countries of prosecutions for witchcraft originating in the evidence of disturbed or atten-tion-seeking children. But sometimes children became the objects rather than the initiators of accusations, or they incriminated themselves, perhaps unintentionally, by claim-ing that certain adults had led them into witchcraft. When children at Mohra in Sweden declared in the late 1660s that some women had taken them to the sabbat, their charges resulted not just in the burning of many women, but also in the execution of fifteen boys aged over 16 and the whipping of forty younger children [5: *207–8*]. Probably the most extreme example of children being punished for witchcraft is offered by the Würzburg scare of 1629. This was a particularly bad example of its species, claiming a total of 160 victims by the close of the year, but it began conventionally enough: only adults were executed in the first few burnings, and these mostly women. Then the pattern changed dramatically, and for a time children made more than 60 per cent of the victims, though this fell back to 17 per cent at the end of the year; it is further noteworthy that in the later stages of this panic, men came to outnumber women among the adults burned [70: *182*].

In most parts of Europe witches condemned to death were executed at the stake, though in England they were hung. Jean Bodin recommended that witches, for the gravity of their offences, should be slowly roasted alive over a fire of green wood, but in practice such extreme rigour was uncommon, and many of the condemned were granted the mercy of strangulation before the fire was well alight. While some authorities took their stand on a reading of Exodus 22:18 (in the King James Bible, 'Thou shalt not suffer a witch to live' – though the sense of the Hebrew word translated as 'witch' is actually quite obscure), some courts were inclined towards greater lenience. The rate of execution of those on trial tended to reach a peak during panics; at other times it was generally rather lower, and even during panics not everyone who was accused of witchcraft was necessarily brought to trial: Midelfort has discovered that during the panic at Mergentheim in southwestern Germany in 1628, only one-third of those denounced as witches were tried [70: *147*]. Table 2 shows the rates of execution of witchcraft defendants in a number of localities.

Defendants found guilty but escaping sentence of death could be punished by imprisonment, flogging, fines or exile; the first of these was often equivalent to a death sentence because of the deplorable state of prison conditions prevailing in the sixteenth and seventeenth centuries. Acquittal rates varied greatly through space and time. Where torture was used ferociously, as at the height of many scares, acquittal was rare, though occasionally a defendant might be released where the evidence was deemed insufficient to establish a verdict, the court retaining the right to restart the trial if new facts came to light. In more normal circumstances of witch prosecution, acquittal was much less unusual. At Essex Assizes, 52 per cent of defendants were acquitted or had their

Table 2: The percentage of defendants at witchcraft trials executed

Location	Executed (%)	Location	Executed (%)
Mergentheim (1628 panic)	93	Poland (1701–50)	46
Pays de Vaud	90	Walloon areas of	41
German-speaking Luxembourg	90	Luxembourg	
		Moscow (seventeenth century)	32
Namur	54	Essex	26
Imperial Free Cities (average)	<50	Geneva	21
Dept. du Nord	49	England (Ewen's	15
Channel Islands	46	estimate)	
		Poland (sixteenth century)	4

Sources: [21, 59, 70, 74, 78, 111].

cases dismissed, and an identical statistic is supported by the limited information available about trials in seventeenth-century Moscow [59; *57*; 111: *1196*]. The acquittal rate at trials in the High Court of Scotland ran at around 50 per cent, and it could reach this figure in a locality in the final stages of a panic, as at Mergentheim in 1630–1 [53: *119*; 70: *149*]. Defendants' chances of acquittal naturally reached a maximum when the jurisdictions trying them or reviewing their cases became sceptical as to the reality of the crime of witchcraft. In England, for instance, Sir John Holt, from 1682 to 1710 Chief Justice of the King's Bench, acquitted all those accused of witchcraft who came before him – probably between twelve and twenty persons [50: *365*]. Given a continuing high rate of acquittal, the practice of prosecution inevitably fell into a decline followed, after a greater or lesser interval, by the formal repeal of anti-witch legislation. Thus before the 1604 witchcraft statute was repealed in 1736, no witch trial had been held in England for nineteen years, and no one had been executed as a witch for forty-three.

[iv] White magic and the law

White magic posed a problem of considerable difficulty for the jurists of early modern Europe. On the one hand, many theologians and demonologists argued for the demonic nature of all magic, white or black, high or low; and if their view was correct, then all practitioners of magic, and not just black witches, deserved harsh punishment for their relations with the Devil. On the other hand, it seemed hard to treat those who employed magic for beneficent purposes in the same way as the witches who were consumed with hatred for God and mankind. A common exit from this dilemma was to enact stiff laws against white magicians but to neglect, from policy or conscience, to apply them rigorously against offenders; in this way the practice of magic was officially discouraged while magicians with good intentions escaped the worst penalties incurred by those with bad. In Monter's words, the bark of law codes in respect of white magicians was worse than the bite of law courts [76: *171*].

White witches, especially those of the lowliest status, nevertheless ran some risk of being taken for black, and during phases of avid witch prosecution must frequently have been punished as such. Those of higher status, being at a greater remove from the stereotype of the maleficent witch, were in less danger, but still needed to be cautious. Some hard-line opponents of magic, such as Bodin or King James, thought that the more knowledgeable magicians were, the more they deserved punishment, for the more fully aware they should be of the iniquity of their activities. For such theorists, Shakespeare's Prospero would have been a more objectionable figure than the three weird sisters from *Macbeth*; but this view would not have been shared by the large number of people of all ranks who believed that magic applied to good ends was legitimate when more conventional methods of problem-solving were ineffectual. By and large, the lack of public revulsion against white magic is reflected in the restraint with which laws against it were in practice applied.

The truth is that magic which was not obviously demonic in its working served the perceived interests of too many people to be readily given up in response to theological

31

scruples. Like its sister occult science, astrology, with which it shared the principle that events in the stars cause sympathetic results on earth, magic appeared too useful a tool for worldly survival and success to be lightly abandoned. Many of the humbler magical operators doubled as astrologers, claiming the ability to read fates in the heavens, and it was natural for a client whose predicted future was unfavourable to seek magical aid in averting it. Many people, of all classes, took astrological advice before making important decisions, and such astral magic as the wearing of charms and talismans carved with astrological signs was common. Great princes, as well as humble folk, sought the services of astrologers and magicians, and many kept their own private consultants. Some magicians travelled widely and acquired international reputations. The famous Elizabethan astrologer and magician John Dee, who was asked to name an astrologically auspicious day for the Queen's coronation, later journeyed to Prague to consult with the Emperor Rudolf ii, a keen student of the occult sciences. Nor was it only secular rulers who exhibited a favourable interest in magic. Even popes, on occasion, relaxed their opposition to it. In 1493 Alexander vi absolved Pico della Mirandola from the condemnation of his views on magic issued by the preceding pope, Innocent viii, while in the seventeenth century Pope Urban viii seems himself to have practised high magic in the company of the philosopher and magus Tommaso Campanella [107: 205–7].

But magic involving the raising of evil spirits or the spirits of the dead continued to attract general disapprobation, whatever its ends. Occasionally a magician was suspected of attempting to raise bad demons, and he might be punished for this, as was Edmund Hartley, executed in 1597; but it is unlikely that many felt much motivation to make such perilous and difficult experiments. While conjuring spirits was 'a fashionable temptation for undergraduates' at Oxford in the earlier seventeenth century [99: 268–9], it was left mainly to such charlatans and showmen as the notorious Doctor Faustus to make large boasts to have spirits at their command (on Faustus and the Faust legend, see [10]).

But if overtly demonic magic was uncommon, orthodox ecclesiastical opinion persisted in seeing the Devil's hand in magical operations in general, and urged their suppression. In response to pressure from both Catholic and Protestant authorities, laws against magic were strengthened in many countries during the course of the sixteenth century, and white magic became a crime where hitherto it had not been one. In 1532 the *Constitutio Criminalis Carolina*, the law code of the Empire, regarded white magic as an offence, but not a capital one. The Saxon code of 1572 was harsher, laying down death as the penalty for white as well as black witchcraft. But even where death or long terms of imprisonment were the statutory punishments for white forms of magic, the full rigour of the law was rarely applied, and Europe saw very few executions for white witchcraft [cf. 76: *171*]. In England, where death was the technical penalty after 1604 for those found guilty a second time of practising white magic, there is no evidence of harshness being the rule in practice, and cunning men and women ran a much greater risk of incurring light penalties in the Church courts than heavy ones in the secular [see 99: *292–5*].

3 The Dynamics of Witch Prosecution

[i] The explanatory task

There is a natural tendency, when contemplating the horrors of witch prosecution in Europe, to consider it to have been a monstrous aberration from the forward progress of Western civilisation, and an extraordinary collective departure from sanity. Phrases like 'witch-madness' (Lea) and 'witch-craze' (Trevor-Roper) come readily to the tongue, and it is easy to sympathise with the view of Robbins that this persecution of elderly women represented 'the blackout of everything that *homo sapiens*, reasoning man, has ever upheld' [87: 3]. Yet such responses, while understandable, hinder rather than help our understanding of the early modern concern with witchcraft. The historian neglects at his peril the somewhat obvious fact that human beings at different times and places see the world in different ways. The possibility demands serious consideration that the prosecution of witches was a rational activity given the complex of ideas and circumstances obtaining in the sixteenth and seventeenth centuries.

Most recent historians of witchcraft have been less concerned to pass adverse judgements on the intelligence or integrity of witch judges and prosecutors, than to analyse the social and intellectual conditions that provided the essential dynamic of prosecution. There is a host of questions which need to be answered here. Why did the prosecution of witches reach a climax in the sixteenth and seventeenth centuries, and what caused some areas of Europe to be more badly affected than others? Why were mainly lower-class people prosecuted, and why were most of these women? How important to the initiation, form and outcome of trials were ecclesiastical, legal and governmental institutions? What degree of popular support was there for prosecution? How significant in starting and sustaining prosecutions and panics were such socially disruptive forces as confessional strife, class tensions, wars, famines and plagues? To what extent did some people genuinely think of themselves as witches and attempt to practise black witchcraft, and what made them do so? These, and other, questions have received much attention in recent years, though many of the answers proposed have proved contentious.

If historians are still some way from consensus about the driving forces behind witch prosecution, the progress of research has at least made some once popular views increasingly untenable. It is, for instance, very unlikely that financial greed played much of a part in stimulating prosecutions, as the influential German scholar Soldan suggested at the end of the last century [96], and several noted subsequent writers have believed. It is true that in some places a convicted witch's possessions were subject to confiscation by the state or civic authorities, and that fees were payable to judges and other court officials, torturers and executioners; and occasionally, too, a professional witch-hunter like the notorious Balthasar Ross at Fulda was motivated by the hope of gain. But on the whole accused witches were too poor to provide rich pickings, and those who accused them were not generally in any position to benefit from confiscations, though they might have to stand the high costs of the legal process. Even when in the course of panics wealthier persons came to be prosecuted, authorities seem to have been remarkably restrained in seizing their goods, and some cities that held panic trials rejected confiscation altogether [70: *165–77*; cf. 64: *113*; 53: *115–16*; 93: *81–9*].

Other casualties of recent scholarship are some highly speculative interpretations of witchcraft and its prosecution that can be shown to be wholly devoid of proper evidential backing. One such is Jules Michelet's mid-nineteenth-century thesis that beleaguered peasants, in protest against repressive social conditions, formed a Devil-worshipping sect and celebrated black masses, thus inviting stern measures of control from the authorities [67]. Another, and even more discredited, interpretation is that of the Egyptologist Margaret Murray, who proposed, with staggering disregard of the requirements of proof, that witchcraft was the true religion of the people until after the Reformation, that the Roman fertility god Janus or Dianus was at the centre of this cult, and that the deaths of such figures as William Rufus and Joan of Arc were really ritual sacrifices to ensure renewal of the crops [79]; the manipulation of evidence that underlies the fantastic structure of Murray's theory has been well exposed in [14].

A view along different lines, but likewise based on a cavalier and partial reading of the evidence, is that tendered quite recently by Ehrenreich and English, who regard the suppression of witchcraft as, above all, the male suppression of women healers [23]. It was women, they argue, who had traditionally been healers among the peasantry; but Church and state believed that only men should be allowed to practise medicine, and accordingly took extreme measures to extirpate their female rivals. Sabbats, at which hundreds or thousands of women met, were real enough, but were merely 'occasions for trading herbal lore and passing on the news' [23: *28*]. This theory, while far from outrageous in claiming that misogyny played a role in the prosecution of witchcraft, falls down on a number of serious counts: it cannot explain why the pressure for prosecution often came from the peasantry itself, and it is silent about the fear of *maleficium* which is well attested by the surviving records of peasant testimony at trials; nor can it account for the prosecution of a substantial minority of *men* as witches. Like Michelet and Murray, Ehrenreich and English have tailored the evidence to fit their favoured theory.

Fortunately there have been several more illuminating theories about the dynamics of witch prosecution. Some of these have been delivered in the course of regional studies of witchcraft, and offer suggestions as to why patterns of prosecution varied from place to place – why, for instance, some areas saw epidemics of witch-hunting whereas others experienced endemic prosecution but few or no panics. A problem with some of the proffered explanations is that they display insufficient sensitivity to the distinction between the intended and the non-intended effects of prosecution, with the result that they leave the motives that underlay it unclear. It may be true, for example, that a community that prosecutes witches in its midst clarifies and reinforces its moral boundaries, by exhibiting in a singularly dramatic manner what it considers to be unacceptably deviant behaviour; and a community which behaves in this way may thereby achieve a stronger sense of its own identity [25, 6]. Yet it is not obviously correct to say that an *intention* to attain this end, socially beneficial though it may be, provided the actual motivation for prosecuting witches – the peasant who accused a woman of maleficent sorcery against him, or the judge who tried her for illicit dealings with the Devil, were thinking of other things than the improved definition of their community's moral norms.

A possible counter to this response is to say that the systems of ideas on which both peasant and judge drew may themselves have been created as a result of the society's need to clarify its own identity by defining its moral limits. Such claims as this are notoriously difficult to evaluate, and an adequate investigation of the view that belief systems arise primarily to serve social imperatives would take us too far from our present subject into deep and controversial areas of sociological theory. What we can reasonably demand, however, is that authors who offer hypotheses about the effects of witch prosecution in sustaining, reinforcing or assisting in the evolution of social rules or arrangements, are not entitled to assume in the absence of argument that such effects were intended ones, and that their attainment provided the motivation for prosecution. Those who claim to explain the dynamics of prosecution by reference to certain social functions it allegedly served, need to show in detail how such social objectives could become translated into the ostensibly quite different rationales which peasants, prosecutors and judges would themselves have offered for their activities.

[ii] Some explanations of witch prosecution

Among the numerous approaches to explaining the stimulating conditions of witch prosecution, four merit some special consideration here.

37

[a] Witch prosecution as a reaction to disaster

Few if any writers have argued that all prosecutions for witchcraft are to be seen as responses to disaster: the implausibility of such a thesis is clear from the experience of England and other regions, which had trials in periods free from war, famine or pestilence. Yet historians have sometimes been struck by the rough temporal coincidence between energetic phases of witch prosecution and natural or man-made disasters. We saw that peaks of prosecution were reached in the last years of the sixteenth century, the period around, and especially just before, 1630, and the 1660s. It is therefore interesting to note that the 1590s and 1620s saw particularly poor harvests, that bubonic plague made a devastating assault on Europe in the years about 1630, and that war and the fear of war troubled the Continent in the last decade of the sixteenth century, the 1620s and the 1660s. Intriguing though these coincidences are, it has not proved possible to discern any significant causal relationships between disaster and witch prosecution. Occasionally, it is true, sorcery was blamed for the incidence of plague; Geneva executed as many as eighty people in the sixteenth and seventeenth centuries for spreading plague in this way [76: *44–9*]. To blame a witch for the onset of a sickness is to follow a pattern familiar to anthropologists, who have recognised the function of witch beliefs in providing an explanation of evil and suffering (see, for instance, [63: *ch.1*]). But there are limits to the responsibility for trouble which can reasonably be placed on witches, and there is no evidence that people looked to witchcraft to explain a rise in the price of bread, or the arrival of an invading army.

Furthermore, a careful scrutiny of the records reveals that the coincidence of disaster and the busiest phases of witchhunting is not quite as close as it first appears. It may be, as Midelfort suggests, that in southwestern Germany war and famine had a destabilising effect which encouraged witch prosecution in the 1620s; but the same author also notes that in the 1630s witch-hunting was declining here, though that decade saw the worst onslaughts on this region of the Thirty Years' War, coupled with plague, famine and economic hardship [70: *121–5*; cf. 93: *89–95*]. Franche-Comté, similarly, had very few trials in the years 1635–44 when it was most badly affected by the war: 'peacetime pursuits like witch-hunting', Monter has remarked, decreased greatly here, as elsewhere in the Empire, during the worst war years [76: *81*]. The case for any direct causal connection between disaster and witch prosecution therefore remains weak; major catastrophes may sometimes have exacerbated the kinds of socially tense situations within which accusations of witchcraft were found convincing, but there is insufficient basis for claiming that witch prosecution was a method of responding to disaster.

[b] Witch prosecution as a weapon of confessional conflict

A different explanation of prosecution is that it was above all a device employed by parties to the savage confessional disputes of the early modern era for quelling religious opposition. The chief protagonist for this view is Trevor-Roper, who has argued that both Catholics and Protestants found it useful to tar their opponents with the brush of witchcraft in order to demonstrate their own godliness. In particular, 'Whenever the missionaries of one Church are recovering a society from their rivals, "witchcraft" is discovered beneath the thin surface of "heresy"' [102: *119*]. To be a Protestant in a Catholic territory, or a Catholic in a Protestant, placed one at risk of being charged with witchcraft in the no-holds-barred struggle between the opposed confessions.

This view has found few supporters. While, as we shall see, there are some grounds for associating witch prosecution with church and state concern to establish their authority over the populace, there is an absence of evidence that Catholics normally prosecuted Protestants, or conversely. It is certainly conceivable that prosecution could on occasions have played the role ascribed to it by Trevor-Roper, but there is no evidence that it always, or even often, did so. Trevor-Roper notes in support of his thesis that witch prosecution increased in the Empire in the late 1620s, coincidentally with the ascendancy of the Catholic forces; yet the records provide no basis for concluding that the prosecutions of those years were an attack on Protestantism [102: *82–3*; cf. 93: *93–4*]. Witch trials happened in many places where there was no, or little, inter-denominational strife, and where the dominance of one church was stable and assured (e.g. Essex, lowland Scotland, Geneva, Venice, the Spanish Basque country). Cases are even known, for instance in the Empire, of adjacent Catholic and Protestant lands exchanging information about putative local witchcraft activities, and extraditing fugitives who had crossed the border to avoid standing trial in their own country. Finally, the Trevor-Roper view ignores wholly the fact that many prosecutions were stimulated not by religious or secular authorities, but by popular demands for action against maleficent magic. The peasant who accused an old woman of harming him by witchcraft was not engaged in the business of confessional strife, and can have cared little to what religious denomination his alleged witch belonged.

[c] Functional explanations

Some historians, inspired by work in anthropology, have sought to throw light on European witch prosecution by identifying positive social functions that it played in communities in which it occurred. When offered as *explanations* of why witch prosecution took place, views on its social benefits face, as we have seen, the task of showing that the achievement of such benefits was really a motivating objective, and not merely a fortuitous consequence, of prosecution. Functional explanations of witch prosecution in Europe are most convincing when they relate prosecution to social or psychological needs of a sort that could hardly have been better satisfied by other means, and that can therefore with some plausibility be regarded as among its stimulating conditions.

Fieldwork in twentieth-century non-Western societies has indicated that witchcraft accusations can sometimes be instrumental in releasing dangerous social tensions, or facilitating the ending of personal relationships which have, for some reason or other, become insupportable. Mayer has suggested that accusations often arise when people find that they ought to feel well-disposed to others but do not, and require a means of breaking an unbearable relationship [66: 62–3]. Kluckhohn's researches among the Navaho Indians show that the making of witchcraft allegations can serve to crystallise, and so release, a variety of social anxieties and uncertainties, and that the very threat of accusation can play a regulatory role, by keeping 'agitators' under control, or by inhibiting people from trying to become too wealthy at the expense of their neighbours [51: *255–7*]. Even the fear of witchcraft can play a useful role in some settings. The worry that a neglected old person may take revenge by sorcery may secure him better care and attention in many societies. Among the Effutu of Ghana, women often accuse themselves of witchcraft in order, apparently, to gain greater respect from their communities [32: *132–9*].

It is an intrinsically cogent hypothesis that witchcraft lore and witchcraft accusations sometimes served similar functions on the European scene. The work of Thomas and Macfarlane on English witchcraft has been important in revealing the stresses and anxieties at village level which typically underlay the making of accusations [99, 59]. Those who invited the charge were generally unpopular on account of their loud and aggressive natures, their inability to get on with their neighbours, and their constant begging – in short, they were the kind of people with whom the average villager would seek to have as little to do as possible. The breaking point in relations with such folk often seems to have been reached when they had demanded, and been refused, charity, and had gone away cursing; in these circumstances there was probably often a very real conviction that any misfortune subsequently occurring to the objects of their anger was due to their witchcraft, though Thomas and Macfarlane have also suggested that those with a guilty conscience for refusing assistance may often have sought relief by trying to convince themselves that the refused beggar was a wicked witch, unworthy of charity [99: *673–4*; 59: *196*]. When in 1645 Mary Edwards of Framlingham, Suffolk, asked Marianne May for some milk and was given less than she wanted, she departed muttering; later a child of the house became lame and died. Mary Edwards was charged with murdering him by witchcraft. Similarly, Emma Gaskin of Newcastle-upon-Tyne in 1667 was refused charity by the maid of Margaret Sherburne, and expressed the wish that 'either she would break her neck or hang herself before night'. Unfortunately for Emma

41

Gaskin, the maid was that night seized with fits, and had a vision of the beggar woman going through the door – a classic illustration of bad conscience leading to a witchcraft accusation [28: *287, 403*].

Thomas and Macfarlane also suggest that such accusations assisted the transition from a state of society in which neighbourly values were highly ranked, to one in which the dispensation of charity became more institutionalised and impersonal, and individual begging grew to be frowned upon [99: *672ff.*; 59: *chs.11, 16*]. It is, however, more likely that the making of accusations performed this function by accident rather than by intention; the promotion of a process of social change can hardly have been the motivating consideration behind the charges laid by Marianne May or Margaret Sherburne's maid. And there are many examples of accusation that do not fit the pattern regarded by Thomas and Macfarlane as normal, and that have no obvious bearing on any processes of social change. In a period when people looked for personal explanations of accident or illness (as many still do in non-Western cultures), it was natural to seek for a witch when trouble came. When John Soam's harvesting cart overturned two or three times on the same day in 1664 as it had collided with the window of Rose Cullender's house, Soam suspected Cullender of bewitching it in a spirit of revenge. In like manner, Richard Edwardes of Suffolk in 1644 lost a child and two cows by mysterious illnesses, and inferred that they had died by the black arts of two women, Anne Leach and Elizabeth Gooding, who had dwelt near the places where the illnesses struck [28: *351, 274*]. Such cases as these were common, and show that by no means all accusations arose from circumstances in which charity had been requested and refused.

The ideas of writers like Thomas and Macfarlane, while some of their emphases may be questioned, have been salutary in directing historians' attention to a hitherto somewhat neglected topic, the popular experience of witchcraft and the role of lower-class people in stimulating prosecutions. Granted the considerable difficulties in the way of recovering the nature of popular consciousness, the drives, ambitions, hopes, fears and anxieties of ordinary folk in the early modern period (for peasants do not write books), the Thomas–Macfarlane approach gives a useful reminder that witch prosecution was not simply the preserve of the upper, literate classes. The reconstruction of the psychology of the sixteenth- and seventeenth-century peasantry, while it will inevitably remain to a degree tentative and impressionistic, is an indispensable ingredient in a general theory of European witchcraft.

Functional accounts which represent witchcraft accusation as aiding in the readjustment of relationships, the releasing of anxieties, or the regulation of social positions, show that accusation could have positive benefits for a community, however dire its effects on the unfortunate accused. Nevertheless, much witch prosecution in Europe was evidently quite dysfunctional: the witch scares which beset many localities in Continental Europe and Scotland were socially damaging not just in causing the deaths of many innocent people, but also by creating extensive public fear and mistrustfulness. A reasonably typical example is the scare at North Berwick near Edinburgh in 1590/91. This began when Geillis Duncane, a servant girl, was suspected of witchcraft, and under torture named a large number of people as associated with her in a witch society. Among those arrested on Duncane's testimony were some women of hitherto unblemished reputation, a schoolteacher named John Fian, and Robert Grierson, a skipper. In the course of the interrogations fantastic tales emerged of dancing with the Devil in the churchyard at North Berwick, and of attempting to raise a storm to drown King James VI at sea at the instigation of Francis, Earl of Bothwell, a powerful and turbulent nobleman. Although not all the fates of the victims of the scare are known, it is clear that several were executed, while Bothwell, who was arrested but escaped from his imprisonment, was forced to flee abroad. It may be concluded that whatever functional roles witch prosecution could sometimes play, it was patently an activity that could get out of hand when taken up enthusiastically by a literate elite armed with the stereotype of the Devil-serving witch, and willing to employ torture to obtain confessions.

[d] Witchcraft and social control

Some writers, impressed by the part played by religious and

secular authorities in the staging of witch trials, have argued that witch prosecution was largely an instrument of social control, a method employed by the powerful to extend or consolidate their hold over the weak. In a Europe racked by religious disagreements which often spilled over into war, the preservation of populiar obedience and loyalty was of urgent concern to states and churches alike, and no measures were spared to secure a religious conformity that seemed to many to be an essential bulwark against social disintegration. Secular rulers found themselves invariably drawn into the contending churches' struggle for dominance, and lent their weight to energetic campaigns to instruct the populace in the principles of the church of their choice, and to suppress, by violence if necessary, anything that smacked of deviation from the prescribed norm. In such circumstances, the practice of village witchcraft, which had for centuries seemed too insignificant a phenomenon to merit much official concern, came to appear as an unsightly and intolerable blemish on the landscape of rural life, and a clear target for extirpation.

This view of witch prosecution has been suggested by, among others, Larner and Elliott [53: *195–6*; 24: *94*], but it has been developed in most depth by Muchembled [77]. Following Delumeau, who had argued that the true Christianisation of the European peasantry did not antedate the Reformation and Counter-Reformation [19; cf. 99: *chs.2, 3*], Muchembled describes the suppression of sorcery as one aspect of a vigorous programme by the authorities to discipline the faith and morals of the people into conformity with a strict Christian blueprint [77: *208ff.*]. The 'submission of souls' aimed at in this campaign was a step towards the centralisation of power and absolutism, and where resisted, or felt to be progressing too tardily, was liable to be pressed forward by drastic means. At local level, Muchembled agrees that pressures such as those described by Thomas and Macfarlane could sometimes stimulate accusations of witchcraft; but he suggests that better-off villagers who were shrewd enough to realise in which way the wind was blowing would denounce witches in order to demonstrate their allegiance to the officially approved virtues of their society, and thus win favour from the authorities [77: *327*].

There is much that seems plausible about this theory of witch prosecution. The rival churches' struggle for the hearts and minds of the people, and the insistent claim of each to be the sole avenue to salvation, sustained a climate in which any dubious dealings in the occult would have been viewed with disfavour. Moreover secular rulers, whether as sincere adherents to a particular church, or as opportunists with an eye to the political advantage to be derived from their subjects being of a single religious persuasion, were naturally keen to assist in the imposition of conformity. Yet there are problems with the social control theory as it stands. It does not, for one thing, cope well with the fact that magic of the white variety was in general dealt with in a relatively mild way by the authorities. Nor does it make it easy to understand why witchcraft had not attracted much more repressive treatment during the Middle Ages, when the medieval Church had hotly and effectively pursued religious deviation, with or without the active cooperation of secular princes. If conformity and obedience mattered to the ecclesiastical authorities as much in the medieval as in the early modern era, why had village witchcraft been left largely alone for many centuries? A likely answer to both these difficulties is that it was only at the close of the Middle Ages that the horrendous stereotype of the Devil-worshipping, sabbat-attending witch appeared, and that it was witchcraft conceived in this new way that attracted the strong repressive measures. But Muchembled is prevented from making this response by his belief that it was traditional witchcraft, rather than demonic witchcraft, that was genuinely under attack in the sixteenth and seventeenth centuries, and by his apparent reluctance to ascribe to the authorities a sincere belief in the reality of the demonised witch; the claim to be battling against the religion and kingdom of Satan he represents as a device of the authorities for installing religious conformity and absolute government [see, e.g. 77: *308*].

Muchembled in fact gives the impression that witch prosecution was a thoroughly cynical and insincere affair, whether promoted by the religious and secular elites eager to control the bodies and souls of the populace, or by the richer peasants concerned to establish their dominance over their poorer neighbours. Not only does this perspective leave it obscure why witch trials should be specifically an early modern phenomenon: it also paints an excessively black picture of human nature not called for by the historical evidence, which does not support the view that people prosecuted others as witches without really believing in witchcraft. There are other theories that share this latter feature with Muchembled's: Trevor-Roper's, for instance, or the view that witches were prosecuted for financial gain or to boost the self-importance of the local officials, or Harris's extreme form of the social control theory that portrays witches as nothing other than scapegoats selected by a corrupt clergy and a rapacious nobility to take the blame for their own misdeeds and dep-redations, while the real offenders posed as the indispensable defenders of the popular interest [41]. All such explanations discount the avowed justifications of those responsible for prosecutions, and allege darker, more dishonourable motives, cynically pursued.

It is, of course, possible that an individual's motives for accusing someone of witchcraft were not always as pure and just as he himself believed. Psychologists are aware that people's real motives are not always what they think they are, and that they can be driven by unconscious or sub-conscious desires that an internal censoring mechanism pre-vents their admitting even to themselves. Some functional explanations seem, indeed, committed to acknowledging the existence within people of such unrecognised grounds of action. Thomas and Macfarlane's suggestion that a charge of witchcraft might be levelled against an importunate beggar by someone with a guilty conscience to discharge after he has refused her charity falls into this category. Similarly, Boyer and Nissenbaum's interpretation of the Salem witch accu-sations as arising from the resentment against the more for-tunate members of that community felt by some of the less successful, ascribes disgraceful motivations to those who laid the charges which they are unlikely consciously to have enter-tained [7]. Yet such explanations do not imply that witch prosecution was a dishonest exercise pursued by people who exploited the existence of beliefs they did not personally share. Rather, they suggest that genuine beliefs were capable on occasion of being utilised in the service of ulterior motives by persons who were unaware of the element of self-deception involved. Even so, such individuals would still have been sincere in the accusations they made; but their wish to find the charges plausible no doubt assisted their ability to do so. It is important to see that admitting that witch prosecution may sometimes have had such grounds is very different from asserting that it was normally the product of cynical self-interest, insincerely masquerading as piety or public conern.

[iii] The genuineness of belief

It may be because witch beliefs are no longer possible for educated Western people that some historians have tended to underrate their role in stimulating prosecution in early modern Europe, and have sought to explain it instead in terms of less time-bound, more universal reasons for human behaviour. Yet most educated men in the sixteenth and for much of the seventeenth century did believe in demons and sorcery, which they thought to be well attested by scripture and the most prestigious ancient writers. Bodin was particularly impressed by the fact that poor and ignorant people accused of magical practices confessed to doing the same sorts of thing as were reported by Plutarch, Herodotus, Philostratus and other ancient authors whom they could not have read; it seemed, therefore, that Satan in all ages incited men to dishonour God, to harm their neighbours and damn themselves by engaging in such activities. Pious Christians needed to maintain constant vigilance against the Devil's recruitment of allies, and to check his formation of witch sects, which grew like cancers in the hearts of communities.

That the ostensible motives for trying witches were real ones is a virtually inescapable conclusion from a scrutiny of the more detailed trial records. In this connection Delcambre's studies of the psychology of judges and suspects in Lorraine trials are of considerable interest [17, 18]. Lorraine judges appear to have been men of high principle, actuated by a sincere desire for the spiritual welfare of the accused, and willing to use torture partly at least from a conviction

47

that by confessing, a witch took the first step on the road to repentance and salvation. These judges believed that they were 'performing a duty, not only of justice and public good, but also of charity and brotherly correction' [18: 95]. The accused individuals who listened to their sermon-like exhortations to confess and repent were of mixed character. Many were people of bad reputation, and some seem to have taken the opportunity to denounce enemies and rivals, involving them in their own destruction. But an interesting category of suspects made voluntary confessions of witchcraft, while others apparently came to believe that they were witches in the course of the judicial process, possibly persuaded by the homiletic style of the judges and the influence of their surroundings; in some particularly striking cases, suspects who had successfully withstood torture without confessing owned to being witches afterwards. While most of the accused would, no doubt, not have confessed had they not been tortured, several seem to have believed sincerely in their guilt, beseeching their judges to pray for their souls, and thanking them for the trouble they had taken in trying them.

In Lorraine, then, a belief in the reality of witchcraft was shared by judges and defendants alike, and was critical to sustaining the trials. There is no reason to think that Lorraine was atypical in these respects. Learned and unlearned people normally had different primary grounds for concern about witchcraft: the common folk were most worried by witches' maleficent magic, the educated by their relations with the Devil, though there is evidence that learned ideas could sometimes percolate through to the popular consciousness, and elements of the learned interpretation become incorporated in the common view (cf. [39]). But what all classes shared was a belief that witches existed, detestable and threatening creatures bent on harm and full of hatred for decent folk. When pressure for witch trials came from both above and below, as it often did, the results were inevitably deadly.

Once the genuineness of belief is properly recognised, it becomes easier to explain why witch trials were a phenomenon of early modern rather than of medieval times. We have seen that the stereotype of the demonic witch was a product of the end of the Middle Ages, and that it involved the notion

48

of her flying by night to meet with others of her kind at great assemblies presided over by the Devil. But only when such a stereotype was in being did it make sense to worry about witchcraft as an alternative, anti-Christian religion. The medieval Church believed in the existence of white and black sorcery, but it did not perceive this as a threat to its own position because it did not see this traditional witchcraft in terms of an organised, anti-Christian sect. A conspiracy of flying witches, acting under the orders of Satan and dedicated to the hurt and harassment of the Christian flock, presented a challenge of an altogether greater magnitude. The religious authorities of the early modern period, while they disagreed about many things, were at least unanimous about the need to respond to this Satanic threat with the greatest urgency, and secular powers gladly assisted in the suppression of a sect believed to delight in doing what harm it could to civil society.

To view the prosecution of witches as a form of social control is therefore to this extent correct: religious and secular leaders saw organised, demonic witchcraft as a threat to their own authority over the people, and took stern measures to protect their positions. But the mistake lies in thinking that states and churches utilised witch prosecution quite cynically as a device for maintaining their control. Rather, they promoted the prosecution of witches because they believed sincerely that only by asserting their power in this way could they protect religion and society from the destructive onslaughts of the great enemy of God and mankind. The peril of witchcraft could be kept at bay only if the people were maintained in their allegiance to true religion and state authority; and there could be no compromise in the power struggle to be waged against the wily and resourceful master of the witches.

Countries such as England and Russia, in which the fully developed concept of the demonic witch obtained no firm rooting, were spared the worst witch-hunting frenzies that happened in places where witches were held to be a Devil-led sect. Even so, any state which gave legal recognition to the notion of demonic pact, as England and Russia did, could hardly escape altogether from what Larner has well described as ripples from the European cataclysm [53: 22]. All over Europe beliefs in the Devil and his dealings with witches gave rise to new legal machinery for responding to the perceived threat. In many places witchcraft was treated as a *crimen exceptum* – that is, as a crime tried according to a modified procedure that permitted torture to extract confessions, and accepted evidence from persons not normally deemed suitable to testify [54]. Furthermore, the disappearance from all jurisdictions by early modern times of the ancient *talion*, which involved an accuser who failed to prove his charge suffering the same penalty as the accused would have suffered if found guilty, made it much safer to level charges, such as that of witchcraft, that were difficult to prove (on the *talion* see [14: *161–3*]). Any legal system reflects the sense of reality of its operators. In early modern Europe, courts were able to find people guilty of witchcraft because the law-makers and judges believed in the existence of witches.

Belief systems are anchored in time, and are products of the general intellectual, social and cultural features of the societies which give birth to them. Probably beliefs in the existence of a subsociety of people who have infiltrated the greater society in order to destroy it are most readily sustained by people who live in a period of insecurity or rapid transition, in which the reassuring solidity of the familiar social institutions seems under threat. Such was the period of the sixteenth and seventeenth centuries, with their religious and political upheavals. Such, too, has been our own century, which has seen many people afflicted in a similar way with fears of the subversive activities of Jews or Communists. 'He will stop at nothing. His utterly low-down conduct is so appalling that one really cannot be surprised if in the imagination of our people [he] is pictured as the incarnation of Satan and the symbol of evil.' That is not Bodin or Remy or the authors of the *Malleus Maleficarum* talking about the Devil-serving witch, though it is a description in their vein: it is, rather, Adolf Hitler, in *Mein Kampf*, presenting his conception of the Jew. *Plus ça change, plus c'est la même chose.*

50

[iv] Women as witches

Women formed, we saw, 80 per cent of the defendants at witch trials. The reasons for this preponderance of women among suspected witches have attracted much discussion, but conclusions have been difficult to verify. It is not, of course, enough to say that more women than men were tried for witchcraft because the stereotypical witch was a woman; the question is why people found it more natural to associate witchcraft with the female than with the male sex, and to accept the stereotype as realistic.

It has been suggested that clerical celibacy lay at the roots of witch hunting. Trethowan has argued that 'sexual desires when inhibited have a strong and sadistic tendency to become a force of destruction', and that a 'fear-laden rejection of woman rose to a raging campaign of revenge and annihilation against her' [101: *343*]. This hypothesis might conceivably fit the violent anti-feminism of the clerical writers of the *Malleus Maleficarum*, but it is less plausible as an explanation of the general expectation that witches should be women. Not all charges of witchcraft were laid by frustrated celibate clerics, nor were all the treatises on the subject written by them. It is not even true that witchcraft accusations were always brought by men against women; commonly the origin of trials lay in accusations brought by women against other women, and sometimes by children.

There were, however, long-established and influential traditions (of male origin) of the mental and moral inferiority of women. A host of biblical passages proclaimed this message, summed up in the famous description of woman as 'the weaker vessel' (1 Peter 3:7). Aristotle, too, had held that women were inferior to men, blaming this on a defect in the process of their generation. It was even questioned by some writers whether women were really human beings, or whether they belonged to some lesser species. Luther, more magnanimously, praised woman as the most beautiful of God's creations, but thought her in respect of more significant properties as inferior to man as the moon is to the sun (for other views of women in the Renaissance period see [62]). Women were considered to be less rational than men, and less able to restrain their passions. Consequently, they were thought to be more easily persuaded into witchcraft by the Devil, once they had been crossed and were seeking revenge. They were believed, in addition, to have more taste than men for the vile and orgiastic activities of the sabbat. Such, at least, were the views of men about women; how fully women themselves accepted these ideas is uncertain, but may emerge more clearly in coming years as more attention is paid to women's history.

Monter has called the prosecution of women as witches 'that uniquely lethal form of European misogyny', and Larner may have intended a similar diagnosis of witch-hunting in describing it as being 'to a large extent woman-hunting' [76: *17*; 53: *4*]. But there is a distinction between hating women and having a poor opinion of them, and while the lowly reputation they enjoyed may have made it easier for women to be suspected of witchcraft, it is not quite so clear that misogyny proper had much responsibility for witch pros-ecution. Disliking women simply as women, and carrying this to the point of wanting to see them burnt alive, can hardly have been very common. But an opinion of women as pas-sionate, cantankerous and unpredictable creatures was preva-lent enough to create a widespread fear of their being easily recruited into the satanic army of witches.

The fear that women could be readily persuaded into witch-craft may have been joined sometimes to an uneasy con-sciousness that many women in economically or socially dependent positions – those who were advanced in age, poor or solitary – had ample reason to place themselves under Satan's patronage. If it is implausible to suggest that com-munities unscrupulously removed their unwanted members by fabricating witchcraft charges against them, it is not unreasonable to suppose that such charges were frequently found believable against people, and especially women, per-ceived as occupying marginal positions in society. Moreover it can by no means be ruled out that women thus situated did sometimes resort to attempting black magic to improve their lot by frightening others into a more respectful manner towards them (cf. [99: *674*]), or in a spirit of impotent rage against those who refused to accord them charity. Maybe the main reason why far more women than men were accused of being witches was that many more women than men actually attempted sorcery, or invoked the Devil's aid, when they found Christian society deficient in satisfying their needs. For men, there were usually more direct methods for attaining their ends or revenging themselves on their enemies; and it is possible that the complaints of a man against harsh or uncharitable treatment would have been listened to, just because he was a man, more sympathetically than those of a woman. Witchcraft may have held more appeal for women than for men not because, as contemporaries thought, women were more wicked and more easily led than men, but because their social and economic position imposed greater constraints on their possibilities of action.

That many people, of both sexes, did practise the techniques of black witchcraft in early modern Europe, just as people in non-Western societies do at the present day, is exceedingly likely, and gathers support from the evidence preserved in trial records of the many confessions that were apparently sincerely made. That the majority of these would-be witches were women – though it is impossible in the existing state of knowledge to be dogmatic here – is perhaps the real explanation of why women constituted four-fifths of the defendants at trials. This hypothesis, it may be said, does nothing to exonerate men from blame for their treatment of these women. If there is some objective grounding for the identification of witchcraft as a woman's activity, there is much to find fault with in male-dominated societies that drove women to such a desperate measure.

4 Why Did Witch Trials Cease?

With the advent of the eighteenth century, the days of witch trials in Western Europe were drawing to a close, though many years were to elapse before the last convicted witch further east went to the stake. Indicative of changing attitudes was Louis xiv's royal ordinance of 1682 which brought prosecution for *sorcellerie* to an end in France, and substituted new offences of *pretending* to have magical powers, to deal with demons or to divine the future. In 1600 most educated Western Europeans believed that witches existed in considerable numbers and formed a dangerous, Devil-led sect. By 1700 many could have been found in agreement with Thomas Hobbes' opinion that, 'as for Witches, I think not that their witchcraft is any reall power'. Even those whose scepticism did not lead them as far as denying that witchcraft might, in principle, be a 'reall power' often doubted whether it was, in practice, very common. A true witch deserves death, wrote the philosopher Malebranche in 1674, but most folk who fancy themselves witches are simply deluded by their imaginations, and are best treated as insane.

In the new climate of opinion, prosecution for witchcraft, as it required the cooperation of the literate classes, became increasingly rare, despite a continuing clamour for it from the peasantry. After 1700 a suspected witch in Western Europe stood more in peril of a popular lynch mob than of a judicial process followed by execution. Yet the reasons for the changing attitudes of the literate classes are not easy to determine. It has often been observed that between 1600 and 1700 there was little major change in the arguments for and against the existence of a threatening subsociety of witches; but people's estimates of the worth of these arguments underwent a transformation, so that what was found convincing in 1600 was not considered so a century later. To see why witch prosecution was in decline in 1700 we need to explain a subtle shift in the prevailing educated world-view.

(i) Changing beliefs

For those historians of a past generation who saw witch beliefs as products of the most benighted superstition, the end of the trials represented the re-emergence of common sense opposition to the hysterical ravings of demonologists and witch judges. But this was unhistorical history; there was, in fact, no 'common sense' basis on which the Europeans of 1600 could have assured themselves of the non-existence of demonic witchcraft. If we do not believe today in witches and the active presence of the Devil among us, that is because such beliefs do not cohere at all well with the overall picture of the world we now hold, a picture determined in large part by the natural sciences. Our contemporary concepts of 'common sense' are a fruit of this natural science tradition, which was in its infancy in 1600, when the dominating characterisation of reality was still provided by theology. This older outlook differed from our modern by assigning a much larger place in the scheme of things to forces of a personal nature – divine, demonic, angelic – and by picturing the universe as an eternal battleground between good and evil. Within such a frame, the belief in a devilish sect of witches was no offence to common sense but, on the contrary, a perfectly reasonable extension of the accepted ideas.

As the seventeenth century advanced, the old paradigms were gradually giving way to new. In 1700 most literate people saw the world in a much less personalised way than their ancestors had done, and they had abandoned medieval man's anxious sense of being surrounded by invisible spiritual presences. This changing world-view sounded the death knell of many traditional beliefs. If there were no demons, then it followed that there could be no demonic witchcraft. Indeed, without demons there could be no demonic magic of any level, and the elegant ceremonies of the Renaissance high magician that were aimed at capturing the assistance of good spirits were as futile as the vulgar performances of the village witch. The tenets of learned Neoplatonism could not carry conviction any more in the face of the growing naturalisation of outlook; not only demons and planetary deities appeared real no longer, but belief evaporated in the quite central proposition that there was a *spiritus mundi* through which stellar influences were transmitted to earth. If God survived in the new picture, he did so in a modified guise. A new orthodoxy arose which portrayed God as acting through natural forces rather than by supernatural interventions (miracles); he was the divine clockmaker, operating via the natural laws he had imposed on the mechanism he had set in motion. Slowly this more naturalistic world-view took root in the minds of the educated classes, gradually excluding the older, theologically-centred notions.

It would be tempting to suppose that witch prosecution received its death blow from the developing scientific revolution of the seventeenth century that, in the work of such giant figures as Galileo, Descartes, Kepler, Huyghens, Boyle and Newton, was to change so fundamentally the way in which men saw the world. Such a view had some currency even among contemporary writers: thus Christian Thomasius, in an influential treatise published in 1701, praised Descartes for disturbing the 'nest of scholastic fantasies' that had kept the witch hunt alive. Yet the responsibility of the scientific revolution for ending the witch trials can hardly have been great. This was, for one thing, a revolution by degrees, not a sudden assault on men's minds; there was no intellectual equivalent of the fall of the Bastille to drive the world overnight into new modes of thought. Most significantly, the theories of the scientific revolutionaries did not obtain a firm basis in educated consciousness until the age of witch trials was past. The courts that in the second half of the seventeenth century became increasingly reluctant to return guilty verdicts against accused witches were not hotbeds of enthusiasm for the new science; most judges and jurors must have been quite unaware that any scientific revolution was taking place, and there is no good reason to suppose that the ideas of Descartes or of Newton influenced their decisions in any way.

Even to some of the most informed advocates of the new science it was not obvious that mechanistic naturalism was the whole story of things; it was not easy to shrug off all vestiges of older thought patterns, and alchemy, astrology and natural magic for a time continued to exist side by side with the new theories – and often less uneasily than we might have imagined (cf. [104: 99]). The great Sir Isaac Newton himself, discoverer of the law of universal gravitation (itself at first regarded by many as just another occult sympathy), spent much of his time pursuing alchemical researches. Some of these scientific pioneers would not even relinquish the belief in witchcraft. Joseph Glanvil, an early member of the Royal Society and an able apologist of empiricist methodology, published a book in 1681 to urge that experience justifies the belief in spirits, and that witches, who consort with evil spirits, merit condign punishment. Later still, Ezekiel Chambers, editor of the *Cyclopaedia: or an Universal Dictionary of Arts and Sciences* (1728), remained willing to countenance the possibility of witchcraft by the evil eye [99: 772]. Many of the protagonists of the new mechanistic scheme of things admittedly did not believe in the activity of spirits, but they were often reluctant to reject the existence of such traditional marvels as sympathetic cures, or the power of amulets to ward off diseases.

It is a reasonable supposition that both the new directions in science and the changing attitudes of witch courts in the seventeenth century had a common source in the decreasing inclination of the literate classes to see reality as permeated by personal and spiritual forces. The scientific revolution was itself a symptom, rather than the cause, of a very general shift in perspective which occurred in that century. This profound change in outlook represented less the consequence of novel reasoning or newly discovered evidence, than of a shift of temperament towards a fresh confidence that man had the capacity to be master of his own destiny.

Underlying this more optimistic vision of man and his possibilities were several, causally interacting, factors. One of the most crucial of these was the greater stress laid on personal responsibility for action by both Catholic and Protestant churches alike from the sixteenth century; higher moral standards of behaviour became expected from both men and women, and as the individual's power to choose to act well or badly was more fully acknowledged, the visibility of the Devil's role as tempter to sin declined. Significant too in this period was the development of more complex banking, trading and other commercial relationships, which demonstrated man's ability to modify and better the conditions of his existence by cooperative activity. Technological improvement, while falling short of being an industrial revolution, was conspicuous in many fields. Printing was the most dramatic of the new inventions, but there were also considerable technical advances in mining, metallurgy, agriculture and land drainage, ship-building, the manufacture of textiles, weapons, glassware, and in a host of other areas, which were born of, and in turn helped to bolster, the mood of confidence in human capacities (on technological improvements see [46]).

But a world which could be shaped so effectively to human desires by men enjoying a new sense of their natural powers, and a conviction of their status as autonomous moral agents, appeared less and less to be a world shared with angels and demons of superhuman abilities. The Middle Ages had believed in the poverty of human resources, the helplessness of men in a hostile world through which the Devil wandered, seeking whom he might devour (cf. 1 Pet. 5:8). When the eighteenth century dawned, such a sense of the ubiquitous menace of Satan was no longer possible for educated people, and it was increasingly common to regard talk of the Devil as a symbolic expression of the evil tendencies within human beings. In this environment the scientific study of nature flourished; witch prosecution did not.

Total disbelief in Satan and the classic stereotype of the demonic witch was not essential to the termination of trials – it sufficed that the old ideas should lose their grip on the imagination to the point that doubt became possible. Late-seventeenth-century courts were generally reluctant to convict people as witches not because they were sure that witchcraft was an impossible crime, but because they no longer felt convinced that it actually took place. As doubts grew, it was normal for jurisdictions to increase their demand for conclusive proof of an accused person's guilt, and to question the efficacy of torture as a means of coming by the truth; finally, nothing at all was judged to be adequate evidence that genuine, Devil-assisted witchcraft had taken place. The case of the Parlement of Paris illustrates the degree of caution which a court might exercise when its confidence in the real occurrence of witchcraft was dying but not quite dead. From 1624 there was a right of appeal to this court against all sentences for witchcraft handed down in lower courts within its jurisdiction, and the Parlement generally acquitted the appellants, or reduced their sentences. Relying little on torture itself, it frowned on its use by lower courts, and in 1639 actually condemned to death three lower court officials who had acted with rough justice against two suspected witches [64: *355*; 97: *38*]. In the 1640s the Parlement ceased to prosecute witches itself, and confirmed guilty verdicts from its subordinate courts only where the evidence was of the strongest [64: *362*].

The possibility that justice might miscarry, especially where torture was employed to secure confessions, seems normally not to have been seriously entertained except where belief in the occurrence of witchcraft was already waning. For long it was a standard belief, as King James put it in his *Daemonologie*, that 'God will not permit that any innocent persons shalbe slandered with that vile defection: for then the divell would find waies anew, to calumniate the best'. Later James changed his mind, and took a pride in exposing false accusations of witchcraft (as at Leicester in 1616, where he compelled a young boy to retract accusations which had already cost the lives of nine women); but by then his contemporaries regarded him as sceptical about the occurrence of witchcraft [50: *314ff.*]. Those who believed that real witches abounded, and were an insult to God, trusted, not unreasonably, that the legal process would receive divine assistance, and that God, who presumably wanted witches to be punished, would protect the innocent from false accusation, or at the very least prevent them from giving way under torture and making false confessions of guilt. The sceptics about witchcraft had no such confidence; in their view torture almost invariably produced the wrong answers. 'Oh cruel tyrants, blood-thirsty judges', Weyer apostrophised the magistrates and executioners in 1563, bitterly protesting against the torture of innocent people beyond the limits of human endurance. Seventy years later the German Jesuit Friedrich von Spee, confessor to many persons accused of witchcraft, urged the same theme, at a considerable risk to his personal safety. Of every fifty burnt as witches after admitting the crime under torture, wrote Spee, it is doubtful whether even two are really guilty; and several condemned people had told him that they would rather suffer ten deaths than undergo such torments again. But Weyer and Spee already doubted whether the Devil really needed to seek the alliance of poor and elderly women and others in pursuance of his nefarious ends. As a rule, the evaporation of trust in the efficacy of torture seems not to have preceded the onset of scepticism about witchcraft, but to have followed it as its product.

If there were an exception to this generalisation, it could be expected to lie in the experience of those communities that suffered severe witch scares, where the expanding circle of accusations extracted under torture seriously threatened all social cohesion. Midelfort has suggested that faith in the legal process could be lost, and trials be brought to an end, once people arrived at 'the shattering realization that witch hunts could destroy all sense of community, and all inhabitants as well' [70: *191*; cf. *158*]. Yet the evidence for such a loss of faith in the legal machinery under these circumstances is lacking. The records do not support the thesis that communities in the final stages of a witch panic had generally formed substantial doubts about their legal procedures; and many centres suffered repeated scares, which would be hard to explain if trust in the efficacy of torture had once broken down. Nor was there anything (as Midelfort also suggests) in the accusation of highly placed people during scares logically to compel doubts, given that on the accepted theory that the Devil sought out human allies, prominently placed people would make particularly desirable satanic recruits, being in the best positions to influence affairs.

It may be that witch scares did sometimes come to an end because their disruptive effects became intolerable, and the social cost of further pursuit of witches appeared too much to pay for the elimination of practices that, however reprehensible, were still a lesser threat to the community than a continued hunt. The dislocation of social relationships, the loss of mutual trust among citizens and the disruption of commerce resulting from the enthusiastic pursuit of witches could be considerable – quite considerable enough to motivate the abandonment of the hunt even when no doubts had formed about the efficacy of the procedures for uncovering witchcraft. But on many occasions witch scares must have stopped simply because the supply of suspects dried up. This could happen because as a scare developed, new suspects tortured for the names of accomplices could more readily satisfy their interrogators by naming people already under suspicion than by accusing others whose innocence had not previously been questioned. Thus persons accused of witchcraft, looking for plausible names to supply to their tormentors, would naturally tend to accuse one another; and the momentum of a scare would decline when the authorities began to find that few new accusations were forthcoming. The North Berwick panic is one that seems to have ended in this manner: several of the accused are recorded as having accused each other of witchcraft, and this appears finally to have led the authorities to believe that the conspiracy had been broken.

[ii] Conclusion

The death of Satan was not a sudden event in the history of European culture; it was a slow process, prolonged over many decades, in which the Devil gradually faded from sight, unable to retain a niche in a view of the world with depersonalised foundations. If the scientific revolution was not the cause of the virtual disappearance of witchcraft trials in Western Europe by the early eighteenth century, it was science, as it became more and more deeply absorbed into the fabric of consciousness, that was finally to convert scepticism about Satan and the reality of witchcraft into firm disbelief. Popular culture lagged behind learned in adopting the new naturalism and abandoning the tendency always to seek explanations of evil in personal terms, but eventually arrived at the same destination. Slowly killed by disbelief, village white and black witchcraft were near to extinction by the nineteenth century. When in the 1880s the child Laura in Flora Thompson's autobiographical *Lark Rise to Candleford* asked her mother whether there were any witches, she received the answer: 'They seem to have all died out. There haven't been any in my time; but when I was your age there were plenty of old people alive who had known or even been ill-wished by one'.

If demonic magic is no longer something that we in the Western world can accept, neither can we believe in the working of any form of non-demonic magic, high or low. The theoretical basis of magic which operates through the hidden forces of nature is, at its most minimal, a conception of the universe as a system of harmonious relationships among its constituent parts, of such a sort that the performance of certain kinds of symbolic action in one place is able, by calling these harmonies into operation, to create sympathetic effects elsewhere. Such a conception is not compatible with the mechanistic naturalism that is the legacy of the seventeenth-century scientific revolution. For those in 1700 who did not see nature in personal and mystical terms, who were unimpressed by the practice of citing ancient authorities in support of beliefs, and who were increasingly disposed to insist that theories not readily capable of experimental testing should be discarded, magic was a baseless and misguided affair; and while popular magicians continued for some time longer to find a clientele, there were by the close of the seventeenth century few educated people not inclined to view the claims made for magic as factitious.

It is easy, but unjust, to condemn early modern beliefs in witchcraft and magic as the ridiculous creations of disordered imaginations, wholly devoid of any respectable grounding in experience. Such condemnation is inappropriate because it ignores the relatively recent consolidation of those concepts of nature, and of the methodology of scientific enquiry, which enable us to see what was wrong with the beliefs at issue. If someone from a developed society in the twentieth century claims to practise magic, we may justly question his sincerity or his sanity; we do not merely refuse to believe that his magic could work, but wonder how he could genuinely believe that it might. But to apply the same attitudes to a sixteenth-century magician or witch is to employ our standards of rationality anachronistically.

A recognition of the changed baseline from which we now think about reality should guard us, too, from succumbing to the temptation to bridle with moral indignation at the deeds of those responsible for judging, torturing and executing accused witches. Among those men there were doubtless some who took a sadistic pleasure in their dreadful duties, yet the majority acted as they did from a spirit of duty and a concern for the public welfare. The prosecution of witches was a tragically misguided business, but it was motivated in general neither by stupidity nor a liking for brutality. There was, properly speaking, no European 'witch craze', for witch prosecution was a rational enough activity given the mistaken presuppositions that underlay it. And the outstanding savagery with which it was so often conducted is, by a bitter irony, a testimony to the purity of intention of the judges and other officials: for men are least attentive to any restraining voice of conscience precisely when they feel compelled to be ferocious by their principles. Witch prosecution was not 'the foulest crime, the deepest shame of western civilization' (87: 3), but it was something even more depressing – a frightful example of how morally motivated action can lead to massive suffering, and good intentions produce the direst consequences.

Select Bibliography

Modern writings referred to in the text are listed below, together with a selection of further recent works of interest. Some classic demonological texts and treatises on witchcraft and magic have found editors and translators in recent years, but for reasons of space these have not been included here.

[1] Isobel Adam, *Witch Hunt* (London, 1978).

[2] Alan Anderson and Raymond Gordon, 'Witchcraft and the Status of Women – the Case of England', *British Journal of Sociology*, xxix (1978). Argues unconvincingly that the milder rate of witchcraft prosecution in England was a reflection of the higher status of women here.

[3] Alan Anderson and Raymond Gordon, 'The Uniqueness of English Witchcraft: a Matter of Numbers', *British Journal of Sociology*, xxx (1979). A reply to [61].

[4] Sydney Anglo, *The Damned Art* (London, 1977). Useful collection of essays about the early literature of witchcraft and magic.

[5] Julio Caro Baroja, tr. by Nigel Glendinning, *The World of the Witches* (London, 1964). Good general history of European witchcraft.

[6] Albert James Bergesen, 'A Durkheimian Theory of "Witch Hunts" with the Chinese Cultural Revolution of 1966–1969 as an Example', *Journal for the Scientific Study of Religion*, xvii (1978).

[7] Paul Boyer and Stephen Nissenbaum, *Salem Possessed: The Social Origins of Witchcraft* (Cambridge, Massachusetts, 1974). Excellent investigation of the social tensions underlying the 1692 witch scare at Salem in New England.

[8] Robin Briggs, 'Witchcraft and Popular Mentality in Lorraine, 1580–1630' [in 105].

[9] Gene Brucker, 'Sorcery in Early Renaissance Florence', *Studies in the Renaissance*, x (1963).

[10] E. M. Butler, *The Myth of the Magus* (Cambridge, 1948). Describes some famous magi, real and legendary.

[11] Pierre Chaunu, 'Sur la Fin des Sorciers au xviie Siècle', *Annales E.S.C.*, xxiv (1969).

[12] Carlo M. Cipolla (ed.), *The Fontana Economic History of Europe: the Sixteenth and Seventeenth Centuries* (n.p., 1974).

[13] Stuart Clark, 'The Scientific Status of Demonology' [in 105]. Interesting attempt to show how demonology took its place as a science in early modern thought.

[14] Norman Cohn, *Europe's Inner Demons* (London, 1975). Impressive study of the development of the stereotype of the demonised witch.

[15] Elliot P. Currie, 'The Control of Witchcraft in Renaissance Europe', in Donald Black and Maureen Mileski (eds), *The Social Organization of Law* (London and New York, 1973). Argues the (implausible) case that witch prosecution was motivated largely by a desire for financial profit.

[16] Lucy De Bruyn, *Woman and the Devil in Sixteenth-Century Literature* (Tisbury, 1979).

[17] Etienne Delcambre, 'The Psychology of Lorraine Witchcraft Suspects' [in 72].

[18] Etienne Delcambre, 'Witchcraft Trials in Lorraine: Psychology of the Judges' [in 72]. [17] and [18] are translated excerpts from Delcambre's *Le Concept de Sorcellerie dans le Duché de Lorraine au xvie et xviie Siècles* (Nancy, 1949–51), an important regional study.

[19] Jean Delumeau, *Catholicism between Luther and Voltaire* (London, 1977). Interesting on the changing nature of popular religious mentality.

[20] Mary Douglas (ed.), *Witchcraft Confessions and Accusations* (London, 1970). Valuable collection of essays by historians and anthropologists, not restricted to Europe.

[21] Marie-Sylvie Dupont-Bouchat, 'La Repression de la Sorcellerie dans le Duché de Luxembourg' [in 22].

[22] M.-S. Dupont-Bouchat, W. Frijhoff and R. Muchembled (eds), *Prophètes et Sorciers dans les Pays-Bas* xvie – xviie Siècle (Paris, 1978). Important surveys of witchcraft and popular prophecy in the Low Countries.

[23] Barbara Ehrenreich and Deirdre English, *Witches, Midwives and Nurses* (London, 1976). Interesting but unconvincing argument that witches were female healers suppressed by the male establishment.

[24] J. H. Elliott, *Europe Divided, 1559–1598* (n.p., 1968).

[25] G. R. Elton, *Reformation Europe, 1517–1559* (n.p., 1963).

[26] Kai Erikson, *Wayward Puritans* (New York, 1966). Proposes that witch prosecution could assist a community to reinforce its moral boundaries.

[27] E.E. Evans-Pritchard, *Witchcraft, Oracles and Magic among the Azande* (Oxford, 1937). Seminal anthropological study of witchcraft.

[28] C. L'Estrange Ewen, *Witchcraft and Demonianism* (London, 1933).

[29] C. L'Estrange Ewen, *Witch Hunting and Witch Trials* (London, 1929). This and the previous work are pioneering investigations of the records of witch prosecution in England.

[30] Lucien Febvre, 'Sorcellerie, Sottise ou Révolution Mentale?' *Annales E.S.C.,* III (1948). Influential for its suggestion that witch prosecution was not the fruit of mere superstitious credulity.

[31] Thomas R. Forbes, 'Midwifery and Witchcraft', *Journal of the History of Medicine,* XVII (1962).

[32] R. F. Fortune, 'Sorcerers of Dobu' [in 65].

[33] Antonia Fraser, *The Weaker Vessel: Woman's Lot in Seventeenth-Century England* (London, 1984). Has a chapter on witchcraft.

[34] Sigmund Freud, 'A Neurosis of Demoniacal Possession in the Seventeenth Century', *Collected Papers,* vol. 4 (1949).

[35] Henry Friedenwald, 'Andres A Laguna, a Pioneer in his Views on Witchcraft', *Bulletin of the History of Medicine,* VII (1939).

[36] Eugenio Garin, tr. by C. Jackson and J. Allen, *Astrology in the Renaissance: the Zodiac of Life* (London, 1983). Illuminating and scholarly.

[37] G. Geis, 'Lord Hale, Witches and Rape', *British Journal of Law and Society,* V (1978). Argues that courts were much more ready on slight evidence to convict women of witchcraft than men of rape.

[38] E. Gellner, 'The Savage and the Modern Mind', in R. Horton and R. Finnegan (eds), *Modes of Thought* (London, 1973).

[39] Carlo Ginzburg, tr. by J. and A. Tedeschi, *The Night Battles: Witchcraft and Agrarian Cults in the Sixteenth and Seventeenth Centuries* (London, 1983). Interesting for its demonstration of the way in which learned ideas about witchcraft could be impressed upon the peasantry.

[40] Michael J. Harner, 'The Role of Hallucinogenic Plants in European Witchcraft', in Michael J. Harner (ed.), *Hallucinogens and Shamanism* (New York, 1973).

[41] Marvin Harris, *Cows, Pigs, Wars and Witches* (London, 1975).

Argues in a lively but unconvincing manner that 'witches' were framed to take the blame for the depredations of the ruling classes.

[42] R. E. Hemphill, 'Historical Witchcraft and Psychiatric Illness in Western Europe', *Proceedings of the Royal Society of Medicine*, LIX (1966).

[43] Gustav Henningsen, *The Witches' Advocate: Basque Witchcraft and the Spanish Inquisition (1609–1614)* (Reno, Nevada, 1980). Relates how an Inquisitor's growing scepticism stopped the witch trials in the Basque country.

[44] Christina Hole, *A Mirror of Witchcraft* (London, 1957).

[45] Aldous Huxley, *The Devils of Loudun* (New York, 1952).

[46] Hermann Kellenbenz, 'Technology in the Age of the Scientific Revolution 1500–1700' [in 12].

[47] Henry Ansgar Kelly, *Towards the Death of Satan: the Growth and Decline of Christian Demonology* (London, 1968). Useful history of Christian views on the Devil.

[48] Ruth Kelso, *Doctrine for the Lady in the Renaissance* (Urbana, Illinois, 1956).

[49] Richard Kieckhefer, *European Witch Trials: Their Foundations in Popular and Learned Culture, 1300–1500* (London, 1976). Proposes an interesting methodology for distinguishing popular and learned traditions about witchcraft.

[50] George Lyman Kittredge, *Witchcraft in Old and New England* (New York, 1929). Useful, detailed account of ideas and events.

[51] Clyde Kluckhohn, *Navaho Witchcraft* [excerpted in 65].

[52] A. Kors and E. Peters (eds), *Witchcraft in Europe, 1100–1700* (Philadelphia, 1972). Anthology of writings on witchcraft from six centuries.

[53] Christina Larner, *Enemies of God: The Witch-Hunt in Scotland* (Oxford, 1983). Surveys the Scottish scene, and contains some good general discussion of the nature of witch beliefs and witch prosecutions.

[54] Christina Larner, *Witchcraft and Religion: The Politics of Popular Belief* (Oxford, 1984). Reprints several of Larner's articles on witchcraft.

[55] Christina Larner, C. H. Lee and H. V. McLachlan, *A Source-Book of Scottish Witchcraft* (n.p., 1977).

[56] H. C. Lea, *Materials Towards a History of Witchcraft* (Philadelphia, 1939). Monumental survey of writings about witchcraft and magic from medieval to modern times.

[57] B. Lenman and G. Parker, 'The State, the Criminal and the

Community in Early Modern Europe,' in V. A. C. Gatrell, B. Lenman and G. Parker (eds), *The Social History of Crime in Western Europe Since 1500* (London, 1980). Describes the legal traditions inherited by early modern states.

[58] Steven Lukes, 'Some Problems about Rationality', in S. Lukes, *Essays in Social Theory* (London, 1977).

[59] Alan Macfarlane, *Witchcraft in Tudor and Stuart England* (London, 1970). Brings an anthropological approach to the study of English witchcraft, concentrating on Essex.

[60] Hugh McLachlan and J. K. Swales, 'Lord Hale, Witches and Rape: a Comment', *British Journal of Law and Society*, v (1978). A reply to [37].

[61] Hugh McLachlan and J. K. Swales, 'Witchcraft and the Status of Women: a Comment', *British Journal of Sociology*, xxx (1979). A reply to [2].

[62] Ian Maclean, *The Renaissance Notion of Woman* (Cambridge, 1980).

[63] Lucy Mair, *Witchcraft* (London, 1969). Good general survey of anthropological theories of witchcraft.

[64] Robert Mandrou, *Magistrats et Sorciers en France au xviiᵉ Siècle: une Analyse de Psychologie Historique* (n.p., 1968). Important study of witch persecution in France.

[65] Max Marwick (ed.), *Witchcraft and Sorcery: Selected Readings* (Harmondsworth, 1982). Valuable collection of writings, chiefly by anthropologists.

[66] Philip Mayer, 'Witches' [in 65].

[67] Jules Michelet, *Satanism and Witchcraft* (English edition, New York, 1939).

[68] H. C. Erik Midelfort, 'Recent Witch-Hunting Research', *Papers of the Bibliographical Society of America*, lxii (1968).

[69] H. C. Erik Midelfort, 'Were There Really Witches?' in R. M. Kingdon (ed.), *Transition and Revolution* (Minneapolis, 1974).

[70] H. C. Erik Midelfort, *Witch Hunting in Southwestern Germany, 1562–1684: the Social and Intellectual Foundations* (Stanford, 1972). Important study of a region much troubled by witch scares.

[71] Roger Mols, 'Population in Europe 1500–1700' [in 12].

[72] E. William Monter, *European Witchcraft* (New York, 1969). A book of readings selected from classic and modern sources.

[73] E. William Monter, 'The Historiography of European Witchcraft: Progress and Prospects', *Journal of Interdisciplinary Studies*, ii (1972).

[74] E. William Monter, 'The Pedestal and the Stake: Courtly

Love and Witchcraft', in R. Bridenthal and G. Koonz (eds), *Becoming Visible: Women in European History* (Boston, 1977).

[75] E. William Monter, *Ritual, Myth and Magic in Early Modern Europe* (Brighton, 1983). A varied collection of essays.

[76] E. William Monter, *Witchcraft in France and Switzerland. The Borderlands During the Reformation* (Ithaca, 1976). Short but fascinating regional account.

[77] Robert Muchembled, *Culture Populaire et Culture des Elites dans la France Moderne (XVe - XVIIIe Siècles)* (Paris, 1978). Important statement of social control theory of witch prosecution.

[78] Robert Muchembled, 'Satan ou les Hommes? La Chasse aux Sorcières et ses Causes' [in 22].

[79] Margaret Murray, *The Witch-Cult in Western Europe* (Oxford, 1921). Once influential but now discredited account of the significance of European witchcraft.

[80] Venetia Newall, 'The Jew as a Witch Figure' [in 81]. Compares Jews and witches as objects of popular hatred.

[81] Venetia Newall (ed.), *The Witch Figure* (London, 1973).

[82] Wallace Notestein, *A History of Witchcraft in England from 1558–1718* (Washington, 1911; reprinted 1965). Old, but still valuable survey of English witchcraft.

[83] Geoffrey Parker, *Europe in Crisis, 1598–1648* (n.p., 1979).

[84] Geoffrey Parrinder, 'The Witch as Victim' [in 81].

[85] J. D. Y. Peel, 'Understanding Alien Belief-Systems', *British Journal of Sociology*, xx (1969).

[86] Edward Peters, *The Magician, the Witch, and the Law* (Pennsylvania, 1978). Illuminating account of the literary and rhetorical traditions that contributed in the Middle Ages to defining the magician and, later, the witch.

[87] Rossell Hope Robbins, *The Encyclopaedia of Witchcraft and Demonology* (London, 1963). Useful as a source of more or less reliable fact, but somewhat sensationalised, and naïve in its scornful condemnation of witch beliefs.

[88] Rossell Hope Robbins, 'The Imposture of Witchcraft', *Folklore*, LXXIV (1963).

[89] Elliot Rose, *A Razor for a Goat. A Discourse of Certain Problems in the History of Witchcraft and Diabolism* (Toronto, 1962). Interesting work of historical imagination, though many of its conclusions are underevidenced (e.g. wandering scholars as witch-masters in the later Middle Ages). Some sidelights on demonology.

[90] Barbara Rosen (ed.), *Witchcraft* (London, 1969). Selects from the Elizabethan and Stuart pamphlet literature.

[91] George Rosen, 'Psychopathology in the Social Process: 1. A Study of the Persecution of Witches in Europe as a Contribution towards the Understanding of Mass Delusions and Psychic Epidemics', *Journal of Health and Human Behaviour*, I (1960).
[92] Jeffrey Russell, *Witchcraft in the Middle Ages* (Ithaca, 1972). Has some good discussion of the nature of witchcraft, and traces some roots of late medieval notions of witches in earlier notions of heretics.
[93] Gerhard Schormann, *Hexenprozesse in Deutschland* (Göttingen, 1977). Valuable on Germany.
[94] Donovan Senter, 'Witches and Psychiatrists', *Psychiatry*, X (1947).
[95] Wayne Shumaker, *The Occult Sciences in the Renaissance: A Study in Intellectual Patterns* (Berkeley, 1972). Covers astrology, witchcraft, white magic and alchemy.
[96] W. G. Soldan (*et al.*), *Geschichte der Hexenprozesse* (Munich, 1911). Pioneering study, still useful.
[97] Alfred Soman, 'The Parlement of Paris and the Great Witch Hunt (1565–1640)', *Sixteenth Century Journal*, IX (1978).
[98] John L. Teall, 'Witchcraft and Calvinism in Elizabethan England: Divine Power and Human Agency', *Journal of the History of Ideas*, XXIII (1962).
[99] Keith Thomas, *Religion and the Decline of Magic* (Harmondsworth, 1978; orig. edn. London, 1971). Magnificent, encyclopaedic study of religion, magic, witchcraft and astrology in early modern England. It has been widely influential.
[100] Lynn Thorndike, *A History of Magic and Experimental Science* (New York, 1923–58). A multi-volume *opus* summarising a vast number of magical and scientific treatises.
[101] W. H. Trethowan, 'The Demonpathology of Impotence', *British Journal of Psychiatry*, CIX (1963).
[102] Hugh Trevor-Roper, *The European Witch-Craze* (Harmondsworth, 1969). A stimulating general history, if questionable in some of its conclusions.
[103] Philip Tyler, 'The Church Courts at York and Witchcraft prosecutions, 1567–1640', *Northern History*, IV (1969).
[104] Brian Vickers, 'Introduction' to [105].
[105] Brian Vickers (ed.), *Occult and Scientific Mentalities in the Renaissance* (Cambridge, 1984). Collection of essays chiefly on learned thought about magic and witchcraft in the early modern era.
[106] P. Villette, 'La Sorcellerie dans le Nord de la France du XVᵉ

Siècle à la Fin du XVIIe Siècle', *Melanges de Science Religieuse*, XIII (1956).

[107] D. P. Walker, *Spiritual and Demonic Magic from Ficino to Campanella* (London, 1958). Very scholarly, illuminating account of Renaissance theories of magic.

[108] Peter Winch, 'Understanding a Primitive Society', *American Philosophical Quarterly*, I (1964).

[109] Frances Yates, *Giordano Bruno and the Hermetic Tradition* (London, 1964). Provides a readable description of Neoplatonist and Hermetic elements in Renaissance magic.

[110] Frances Yates, *The Occult Philosophy in the Elizabethan Age* (London, 1979). Discusses occultism in the literary tradition, and describes some of the Renaissance magi.

[111] Russell Zguta, 'Witchcraft Trials in Seventeenth Century Russia', *American Historical Review*, LXXXII (1977).

[112] Gregory Zilboorg, *The Medical Man and the Witch during the Renaissance* (Baltimore, 1935). An account of early modern writings on witchcraft from the point of view of psychiatry.

Index